STUDENT UNIT GUIDE

NEW EDITION

AQA AS Accounting Unit 1
Introduction to Financial Accounting

Ian Harrison

Philip Allan, an imprint of Hodder Education, an Hachette UK company, Market Place, Deddington, Oxfordshire OX15 0SE

Orders
Bookpoint Ltd, 130 Milton Park, Abingdon, Oxfordshire OX14 4SB
tel: 01235 827827
fax: 01235 400401
e-mail: education@bookpoint.co.uk
Lines are open 9.00 a.m.–5.00 p.m., Monday to Saturday, with a 24-hour message answering service.
You can also order through the Philip Allan Updates website: www.philipallan.co.uk

ISBN 978-1-4441-7221-8

First printed 2012
Impression number 5 4 3 2 1
Year 2017 2016 2015 2014 2013 2012

Cover photo: Fotolia

Typeset by Integra Software Services Pvt. Ltd., Pondicherry, India

Printed in Dubai

Hachette UK's policy is to use papers that are natural, renewable and recyclable products and made from wood grown in sustainable forests. The logging and manufacturing processes are expected to conform to the environmental regulations of the country of origin.

P02075

Contents

Getting the most from this book

Questions & Answers

Exam-style questions

Examiner comments on the questions

Tips on what you need to do to gain full marks, indicated by the icon **e**.

Sample student answers

Practise the questions, then look at the student answers that follow each question.

Examiner commentary on sample student answers

Find out how many marks each answer would be awarded in the exam and then read the examiner comments (preceded by the icon **e**) following each student answer. Annotations that link back to points made in the student answers show exactly how and where marks are gained or lost.

AQA AS Accounting

About this book

This student guide is an ideal resource for your revision of AQA Accounting AS Unit 1: Introduction to Financial Accounting. The guide is in two sections:
- Content Guidance covers the content of Unit 1.
- Questions and Answers provides ten questions; each question focuses on a specific area of content. Each question is based on the format of the AS examination papers and is followed by two sample answers (an A-grade and lower-grade response) together with comments by the examiner.

You should read the relevant topic area in the Content Guidance section before you attempt a question from the Questions and Answers section. Only read the specimen answers after you have attempted the question yourself.

Aims of the AS qualification

The AS accounting course aims to encourage you to develop:
- an understanding of the importance of effective accounting information systems and an awareness of their limitations
- an understanding of the purposes, principles, concepts and techniques of accounting
- the transferable skills of numeracy, communication, ICT, application, presentation, interpretation, analysis and evaluation in an accounting context
- an appreciation of the effects of economic, legal, ethical, social, environmental and technological influences on accounting decisions
- a capacity for methodical and critical thought which serves as an end in itself as well as a basis for further study of accounting and other subjects

The Content Guidance section of this guide outlines the topic areas covered in Unit 1.

Unit 1 is designed as the foundation for the whole A level course and covers double-entry procedures applied to the accounting systems of sole traders. It deals with how the double-entry system operates and will help you to develop your skills in keeping accounting records.

On completion of the unit you should be able to:
- record a variety of transactions in the double-entry system from source documents and the appropriate subsidiary books and demonstrate an understanding of the double-entry process
- transfer appropriate amounts from the nominal accounts in the general ledger and prepare a statement of financial position in good form from the real accounts and any other relevant accounts
- make adjustments for prepayments and accruals both in the general ledger and to financial statements
- make provision for depreciation in the income statement and statement of financial position using the straight-line method
- verify the accuracy of accounting records and explain the purpose of using verification techniques and appreciate any limitations on their uses
- assess the effect that errors have on profit calculations and on the relevant sections of a statement of financial position

Content Guidance

The Content Guidance section outlines the topic areas covered in Unit 1. Unit 1 is designed as the foundation for the whole A-level course and covers double-entry procedures applied to the accounting systems of sole traders. It deals with how the double-entry system operates and will help you to develop your skills in keeping accounting records.

On completion of the unit you should be able to:

- record a variety of transactions in the double-entry system from source documents and the appropriate subsidiary books and demonstrate an understanding of the double-entry process
- transfer appropriate amounts from the nominal accounts in the general ledger and prepare a statement of financial position in good form from the real accounts and any other relevant accounts
- make adjustments for prepayments and accruals both in the general ledger and to financial statements
- make provision for depreciation in the income statement and statement of financial position using the straight-line method
- verify the accuracy of accounting records and explain the purpose of using verification techniques and appreciate any limitations on their uses
- assess the effect that errors have on profit calculations and on the relevant sections of a statement of financial position

Purposes of accounting

Reasons for keeping accounting records

The owners or managers of businesses keep accounting records in order to record:

- incomes and expenditures during an accounting period
- profits and losses during an accounting period
- the value of and any changes in the values of assets and liabilities
- amounts owed to payables (creditors) and amounts owed by receivables (debtors) and any changes to these amounts during an accounting period

Additionally, records are kept to:

- allow interpretation and comparison of results over different time periods:
- satisfy legal requirements, for example Revenue and Customs
- allow any providers of finance to see that the capital they have invested is being used wisely and is in safe hands

All the above reasons can be summarised under the headings of stewardship and management.

The **stewardship** function of accounting is the use of financial information by the providers of finance to determine how the funds they have provided are being used within the business.

The **management** function of accounting is the use of financial information to provide managers with information that allows them to evaluate performance, highlighting areas of good practice and areas that need remedial action.

Knowledge check 1

Distinguish between the management and stewardship functions of accounting. Explain one example of accounting information being used for management purposes and one example of accounting information being used for stewardship purposes.

Accounting records

Source documents and subsidiary books

Source documents

The financial recording process always starts with a source document. The source document is used to provide the first entry (the 'prime' entry) in the financial records. It is important that you are able to describe the details shown on each source document and the purpose for its issue. You should also be able to write up the appropriate subsidiary book from each type of source document.

The source documents are:
- **purchases invoice** — the document received from a credit supplier demanding payment. It also stipulates any credit terms.
- **sales invoice** — the document sent to a credit customer demanding payment. It also stipulates any credit terms.
- **cheque counterfoils** (cheque book 'stubs') — the record of the details entered on a cheque.
- **paying-in slip counterfoils** — the record of the details entered on the paying-in slip.
- **cash receipts** — the document showing that a certain amount of money has been paid.
- **till rolls** — the record made by a cash register showing all receipts.
- **bank statements** — these also act as a source document. The information provided by bank statements includes:
  - **standing orders** — instructions written by a bank customer asking the bank to pay a fixed amount of money on a regular basis into another account
  - **direct debits** — these allow a business to charge costs to a customer's bank account automatically: the amount can be increased or decreased within certain limits agreed by the customer
  - **BACS** (Bank Automated Clearing System)
  - **credit transfers**
  - **bank charges** — the charges made by the bank for carrying out work for a customer.

It is important that you can define each of the terms used on a bank statement concisely and know how they affect the business's bank balance.

Subsidiary books

There are six subsidiary books that could figure in an examination question. Remember that the subsidiary books are not part of the double-entry system, with the exception of the cash book.

Knowledge check 2

Identify three types of transaction appearing on a bank statement, other than cheque payments and lodgements, that are used as source documents.

Examiner tip

Do not refer to the subsidiary books as 'accounts'. The subsidiary books are the 'starting point' that allows entries to be made in the ledgers.

The **sales day book** is a list of all the credit sales made to customers. Postings are made from the sales day book to the debit of each individual customer's account in the sales ledger. A credit entry is made (by using the total of all the debits entered in the sales ledger) in the sales account in the general ledger. (Remember that the sales day book is not part of the double-entry system.) It is written up from copy sales invoices; the top copy is generally sent to the customer.

The **sales returns day book** is a list of goods returned by customers. The returns are posted individually to the credit of the customer's account in the sales ledger. A debit entry is made by using the total of all the credits entered in the sales ledger in the sales returns account (returns inwards) in the general ledger. It is written up from the copy of the credit note sent to the customer.

Do not enter the sales returns in the sales account. This results in a net sales figure and could mask an 'unacceptable' level of returns from customers.

The **purchases day book** is a list of purchases made on credit. Individual purchases are credited to the appropriate suppliers' account in the purchases ledger. The debit entry in the purchases account in the general ledger is the total of the individual purchases listed.

The **purchase returns day book** lists goods returned to suppliers. Entries are made on the debit side of individual suppliers' accounts in the general ledger. The credit entry in the purchase returns account is made up of the total of all the entries in the purchase returns day book. It is written up from credit notes received from the suppliers.

The **cash book** is the subsidiary book in which all cash and bank transactions are recorded.

The **journal proper** (often referred to as **journal**) is used, at this stage of your studies, for four types of transaction. It is used to record:
- the purchase of non-current assets on credit terms
- the sale of non-current assets on credit terms
- the transfer of entries from one ledger account to another
- the correction of errors that have been discovered in the double-entry system

The use of the journal is necessary because:
- some transactions do not fit comfortably into one of the other subsidiary books
- even unusual transactions must first be entered into a subsidiary book
- it reduces the likelihood of only using one entry in the double-entry system
- as a part of the audit trail, it reduces the likelihood of fraud being perpetrated

There are a variety of source documents used to write up the journal, but the usual ones given in AS examination questions are invoices.

The layout of entries in the journal is important and is unique to the book. An entry in the journal looks like this:

	Dr £	Cr £
Motor vehicles	27 500	
Abcon Motors Ltd		27 500
Purchase of van BC08 DEF from Abcon Motors Ltd		

Examiner tip

You should be able to record the information given on any source document in the correct subsidiary book. This is examined frequently, generally as part of a larger question involving double-entry transactions.

Examiner tip

If you find it difficult to prepare journal entries, try drawing up 'T' accounts, then from these 'T' accounts draw out your journal. The journal should be prepared first, as it is a subsidiary book.

Knowledge check 3

Identify the two ledger accounts that would be prepared from entries in (a) the purchases day book and (b) the sales returns day book.

Double entry

It is essential that you master the basic concept of double entry. The key is always to remember that every transaction is entered twice in the ledger: one entry on the debit side of an account and one entry on the credit side of another account. In businesses that have many credit transactions, the ledger is generally split into three parts:

- the **sales ledger** — this contains the accounts of all customers the business deals with on credit terms.
- the **purchases ledger** — this contains the accounts of all the suppliers the business deals with on credit terms.
- the **general ledger** — this contains all other accounts: nominal, real and liability accounts.

The general rule is that a person's account (or other business's account) is contained in either the sales or purchases ledger, since the business's dealings with people (or other businesses) are as either a supplier or a customer.

So every transaction has two entries. The two entries may be in different parts of the ledger.

Example:

Tony purchases goods for £236 for resale on credit from Catherine.

Prepare the appropriate accounts in Tony's ledger.

Answer:

	Purchases ledger				General ledger		
Dr	Catherine	**Cr**	**Dr**	Purchases account		**Cr**	
	Purchases 236		Catherine	236			

Here is a detailed example of an account taken from a general ledger:

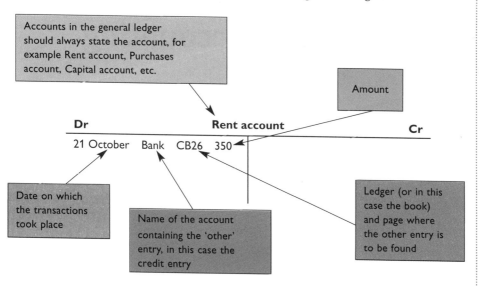

Accounts in the general ledger should always state the account, for example Rent account, Purchases account, Capital account, etc.

Amount

Dr	Rent account			**Cr**
21 October	Bank	CB26	350	

Date on which the transactions took place

Name of the account containing the 'other' entry, in this case the credit entry

Ledger (or in this case the book) and page where the other entry is to be found

Examiner tip

Only personal accounts are found in the sales ledger and purchases ledger. The general ledger contains real accounts and nominal accounts.

Knowledge check 4

Pawar is a credit customer. Her account appears in the sales ledger. True or false?

Knowledge check 5

Explain why a ledger is generally split into three parts.

Examiner tip

If asked to prepare an account, you must provide all the details.

The details help to locate the other entry that completes the double entry. These 'locating devices' help if there is an error in any of the ledgers; they provide an audit trail.

Remember that all entries in the ledger must start their journey through the double-entry system in one of the subsidiary books.

Summary

- All business transactions must first be entered in a subsidiary book before they can be entered in the double-entry system. The recording of all transactions must start with the use of a source document.
- The subsidiary books that record credit transactions are the purchases day book, the sales day book, the purchases returns day book, the sales returns day book, and the journal.
- Each book is a list of similar types of transaction.
- The cash book is a subsidiary book in which all cash and bank transactions are recorded. It is also part of the double-entry system.
- The journal deals with transactions that do not comfortably fit into the other five books of prime entry.
- Subsidiary books are a convenient way of entering transactions into the double-entry system.
- All financial transactions are recorded in accounts; all accounts are found in the ledger.
- Every debit entry in the ledger must have a corresponding credit entry.

- Every credit entry in the ledger must have a corresponding debit entry.
- The ledger is divided into three separate parts since this makes it easier and more convenient to use.
- Credit accounts of suppliers are found in the purchases ledger.
- The accounts with customers who are allowed credit facilities are found in the sales ledger.
- All other accounts are found in the general ledger.
- The accounts found in the general ledger are: nominal accounts, real accounts and liability accounts.
- Debit entries in a ledger account should show the date when the transaction was recorded, the name of the account containing the credit entry, the ledger and page where the credit entry can be found, and the amount of the transaction.
- Credit entries should show the date, the corresponding debit entry with its ledger and ledger page, and the amount.
- You should use 'T' accounts only for personal workings and for solving double-entry problems.

Examiner tip

If there is a balance on any account, always carry it down to start the next time period. If not, you will forfeit a mark *unless* a question tells you specifically not to carry balances down. A debit balance on an account is the balance that has been brought down on to the debit side. A credit balance has been brought down on to the credit side.

A **trial balance** is a summary of all balances extracted from all ledgers.

Verification of accounting records

The trial balance

You should be able to prepare a **trial balance** almost as quickly as you are able to write down the details of each account summarised in the trial balance. The trial balance is extracted from all the detailed accounts in the ledger(s). It is extracted on one day (usually the final day of the financial year) and so the heading tells us this.

Example: **Mary Marshall. Trial balance at 31 March 2012**

On the debit side of a trial balance you should include only **assets** and expenses. Examples include:

Assets	Expenses
Machinery	Rent
Vehicles	Motor expenses

On the credit side of a trial balance you should include only liabilities and incomes/benefits. Examples include:

Liabilities	Incomes/benefits
Mortgage	Sales
Bank loan	Discounts received
Capital	Rent received

It is helpful to remember this by using a mnemonic. (e.g. DRASEX — Dr Assets Expenses; CLIB — Cr Liabilities Incomes/benefits).

There are a few exceptions to the assets/expenses and liabilities/incomes or benefits rule — for example returns and drawings.

Returns inwards (goods previously sold but now returned by a customer, i.e. sales returns) will be on the opposite side of the trial balance to sales. Sales are a credit entry so sales returns must be a debit entry in the account and in the trial balance.

Returns outwards (goods previously purchased but now returned to the supplier, i.e. purchase returns) will be on the opposite side of the trial balance to purchases. Purchases are a debit entry so purchases returns must be a credit entry in the account and in the trial balance.

Drawings by the proprietor cause money (or goods) to go out of a business and should be treated in the trial balance like other transactions that remove money from the business (i.e. expenses). Although the drawings are not a business expense, they are debited in the trial balance.

The trial balance is a summary of all the accounts in all the ledgers. So, an insurance account may look like this:

Dr			Insurance account	Cr
8 January	Bank	127		
13 July	Bank	1386		
2 September	Bank	272		
9 November	Bank	931		

The trial balance would summarise the account and show:

Trial balance at 31 December 2012

	Dr	Cr
Insurance	2716	

The amount shown in the trial balance for trade receivables is the total of all the debit balances extracted from the sales ledger. Clearly, to list each individual balance from each account in the sales ledger on the trial balance for a business with many credit customers would result in a trial balance that might have to be written on a sheet of

Knowledge check 6

Would the following ledger accounts appear in the debit column or the credit column of a trial balance: sales; drawings; carriage outwards; returns outwards; closing inventory; rent payable; discounts received?

Examiner tip

Most trial balances have more debit entries than credit entries.

Knowledge check 7

A trial balance is a list of the assets and liabilities of a business. True or false?

paper as long as a roll of wallpaper. Similarly, to list each credit balance extracted from the purchases ledger could also result in a long list.

Why do people prepare a trial balance? The sole function of extracting a trial balance is to check the arithmetic accuracy of all the entries made in the ledgers. Additionally:

- The trial balance can disclose some errors in the double-entry system before financial statements are prepared. If a trial balance does not balance, the final accounts cannot balance unless there are one or more compensating errors that counteract the discrepancy on the trial balance.
- Using the figures shown in the trial balance is easier than referring back to each individual account in the ledgers.
- It can help to prevent fraud if the ledgers are maintained by someone other than the person responsible for extracting the trial balance.

The six types of error not revealed by extracting a trial balance are:

(1) Commission — an entry is made in an incorrect account of a similar type. For example, a motor vehicles account is debited with an entry that should have been debited to office equipment or the account of Thomas and Son is credited with credit purchases received from Thompson.

(2) Reversal — a debit entry and credit entry is made which should in fact have been a credit entry and a debit entry. For example, goods for resale purchased on credit from Mansoor are debited to Mansoor and credited to the purchases account.

(3) Omission — neither a debit nor a credit entry is made; there has been no record made in the double-entry system. For example, a purchase invoice has been lost, so no entry is made in the purchases day book. As a result, no entry is made in a personal account in the purchases ledger and no entry is made in the purchases account in the general ledger.

(4) Principle — entries are debited or credited in the wrong class of account. This type of error makes both the income statement and the statement of financial position incorrect. For example, a van purchased for use in the business is debited to the motor expenses account.

(5) Original entry — an error is made when entering the information from a source document to one of the subsidiary books. For example, goods valued at £123 sold to a credit customer are entered in the sales day book as £132.

(6) Compensating error — error(s) on the debit side of an account(s) equals error(s) on the credit side of an account(s).

Suspense accounts

When a trial balance fails to balance, the difference is placed in a temporary account called a suspense account. If the debit side of a trial balance is larger than the credit side, insert a 'suspense' item on the credit side so that the debit and credit columns have the same total. If the credit side of a trial balance is larger than the debit side, insert a 'suspense' item on the debit side so that the debit and credit columns have the same total. When you have corrected the errors given in a question, the suspense item is cancelled out and the trial balance will balance.

Some exam questions do not give the original trial balance difference. You may have to calculate this by entering errors in a suspense account. The figures used in the

Examiner tip

You must know the six types of error that are not revealed by extracting a trial balance that balances. You must also be able to describe an example of each type of error. Learn a mnemonic such as CROPOC.

Knowledge check 8

Explain the difference between an error of commission and an error of principle.

Knowledge check 9

What does the mnemonic CROPOC stand for?

A suspense account is a temporary account where any difference in trial balance totals is held until errors are identified and corrected.

suspense account will mean that it does not balance. The 'missing figure' is the amount by which the trial balance did not balance before the errors were corrected.

Remember that the trial balance is a summary of all the balances extracted from all of the ledgers. So if you have to add an extra debit in your suspense account to make it balance, this means that there was a missing debit balance, i.e. suspense account debit balance on the trial balance, before the errors were discovered.

You must be able to adjust gross profit and profit for the year to take into account any errors corrected. Errors requiring adjustments to:
- sales
- purchases
- sales returns
- purchases returns
- carriage inwards

will affect gross profit and profit for the year calculated before the errors were corrected.

Errors requiring adjustments to:
- expenses
- incomes/benefits (discount received, rent received, etc.)

affect profit for the year only.

Errors requiring adjustments to:
- assets
- liabilities

do not affect gross profit or profit for the year *unless* the error is an error of principle, such as a new motor van (£36 000) being included as motor expenses. Correction of this error of principle would cause profits to rise by £36 000.

Bank reconciliation statements

This is a popular topic with examiners. It is less popular with students.

When a business has a current account with a bank, the owners of that business keep a record of dealings using the bank account. The bank also keeps a record of the same transactions in its ledger. The bank sends a copy of its record in the form of a bank statement at intervals agreed with the customer. When a bank statement is received from a bank, a trader compares this copy of the bank's records with his/her own records shown in the bank columns of his/her cash book.

The purpose of preparing a **bank reconciliation statement** is to check the accuracy of the entries in the bank columns of the cash book by using an independently prepared document (the bank statement). The two balances should agree because they are both prepared using the same amounts. However, the balance shown in a trader's cash book (bank columns) may not agree with the balance shown on the bank statement on the same date (see below).

Remember that a debit bank balance given in a trader's cash book shows that a trader has money in the bank, and a credit balance means that the business has an overdraft. However, because a bank statement is a copy of the bank's records, the opposite is true. A debit balance on a bank statement means the account is overdrawn and a credit balance shows that the business has money in the bank account.

Remember that the cash book balance is the one that is used in a trial balance and in a business's statement of financial position.

You should know and remember the reasons why the two balances might not agree.

Possible cash book balance errors

Unpresented cheques are cheques that have not yet been cleared by the bank and therefore do not appear as debit entries on the business's bank statement.

Lodgements are amounts paid into the bank account of a business.

The balance in a trader's books of accounts may not agree with the balance in the bank's records for two reasons:

(1) Time differences in recording transactions:
- When a trader lodges money in the bank, the transaction is recorded immediately in the trader's cash book using the paying-in slip counterfoil as the source document. The bank may not credit the trader's account until a couple of days later.
- When a trader writes out a cheque, it is recorded immediately in the trader's cash book using the cheque counterfoil as the source document. The bank does not credit the account until the cheque is presented for payment.

(2) Lack of knowledge by the trader:
- The bank debits a trader's account with bank charges, interest etc., but the trader remains unaware of the amounts until the appropriate bank statement is received.
- The bank may credit a trader's account with counter credits or payments made directly into the account without the trader's knowledge. The trader may be unaware of the amounts until either a bank statement or notification is received.
- The bank may dishonour a cheque. The trader would be unaware of this until a bank statement or notification is received.

General errors

It is now rare for banks to make the following errors. The major error made by banks is to debit or credit an amount that should be entered in another business's account. Nevertheless, you should be aware of the possibility of:
- casting errors in the cash book
- entering incorrect amounts in the cash book
- entering items on the wrong side of the cash book

Examiner tip

The entries on a bank statement appear to be recorded incorrectly. Money received into the bank account by a business is shown on the bank statement as a credit entry while cheque payments are shown as debit entries on a bank statement. This happens because the bank statement is a replica of the bank's ledger records.

Procedure used to answer a question

In order to answer an examination question, you are generally required to prepare two elements:
- You must update the cash book since this is part of the business records.
- You must then prepare the actual reconciliation statement.

A good procedure to follow is shown on the next page:

(1) Balance the bank columns of the cash book and carry the balance down.
(2) Compare the bank columns of the cash book with the entries shown on the bank statement.
(3) Bring the cash book up to date by:
  (a) entering payments shown as paid by the bank that have not been entered in the bank column on the credit side of the cash book
  (b) entering any amounts received by the bank that have not been entered in the bank column on the debit side of the cash book.
(4) Correct any errors discovered in the bank columns of the cash book. (Remember that, when comparing the cash book entries with the bank statement entries, the bank statement entries are always assumed to be correct.)
(5) If the bank statement contains errors, inform the bank and ask for an adjusted bank statement balance.
(6) Prepare the bank reconciliation statement.

T. Relph. Bank reconciliation statement at 30 June 2012

	£	£
Balance at bank as per cash book		582
Add unpresented cheques		
cheque number 137	42	
cheque number 151	28	
cheque number 165	37	
		107
		689
Less lodgements not yet credited		416
Balance at bank as per bank statement		273

Sales and purchases ledger control accounts

Control accounts verify only the arithmetic accuracy of the entries in the ledger being checked. There could be errors in the control account that remain undetected. These are errors of:

- commission
- reversal
- omission
- original entry
- compensating errors

These errors are the same as those detailed in the errors not affecting the balancing of a trial balance (see p. 12). You must learn them.

The type of error missing is errors of principle. Why would an error of principle not be revealed when you prepare a ledger control account? Answer: an error of principle would be an entry in the wrong class of account in the general ledger. Neither entry would, generally, be entered in a personal ledger.

(see p. 12)

Examiner tip

Learn the layout of a bank reconciliation statement and always use a heading.

Knowledge check 12

A cash book shows a payment to Tompkins £56. The bank statement shows the amount as £65. Which amount is deemed to be the correct amount?

Knowledge check 13

Balance at bank as per the bank statement £890 debit; unpresented cheques £1840; lodgements not yet credited £1470. A standing order not entered in cash book £48.

What is the balance at bank shown in the cash book?

Which is the correct amount to be shown in (a) a trial balance (b) a statement of financial position?

Examiner tip

If there is more than one unpresented cheque, it is safer to list these in the reconciliation statement. If you add them on your calculator and make an error, the examiner cannot award part marks.

Control accounts are used to check the accuracy of entries in each purchases and sales ledger.

Items that appear as both a debit entry and a credit entry in the double-entry system are called **contra items**. They may be found in the cash book of a business and in control accounts. Contra items have no effect on the wellbeing of the business.

Set-offs or contra items

A business may be both a supplier and customer to another business. For example, Ash & Co. sells timber valued at £1200 on credit to C. Hair, a furniture manufacturer. Ash purchases four office desks on credit for £800 from Hair. The entries in the ledgers of Ash would show:

Purchases ledger page 42				Sales ledger page 61			
Dr Hair		**Cr**		**Dr** Hair		**Cr**	
Office equipment	800			Sales	1200		

Note that the descriptions tell us where the opposite entry is to be located. There is a debit entry of £800 in the office equipment account in the general ledger. There is a credit entry of £1200 in the sales account in the general ledger.

It would not be sensible for Ash to demand £1200 payment from Hair and to send Hair a cheque for £800. As the amount due to Ash is greater than the amount owed by Ash, it would seem sensible to set off the amount owed to Ash against the amount owed by Ash.

Purchases ledger				Sales ledger			
Dr	Hair	**Cr**		**Dr** Hair		**Cr**	
Transfer to sales ledger 800				Transfer from purchases ledger		800	

This transaction would be recorded in the journal as the appropriate subsidiary book.

Transfer of credit balance in Hair's account in the purchases ledger to Hair's account in the sales ledger:

Journal			
Hair	PL 42	800	
Hair	SL 61		800

After this transfer, the ledgers would show:

Purchases ledger page 42			
Dr	Hair		**Cr**
Transfer to sales ledger	800	Office equipment	800

Sales ledger page 61			
Dr	Hair		**Cr**
Sales	1200	Transfer from purchases ledger	800

All entries in any personal ledger must also show in a control account. There are:
- debit entry for £800 in Ash's purchases ledger control account
- credit entry for £800 in Ash's sales ledger control account

Knowledge check 14

The debit balance on a sales ledger control account is £18600. It has been discovered that returns inwards £190 have been entered on the debit side of a sales ledger control account. After correcting the error, what are the balances on the control account?

Schedules of trade receivables and trade payables

These are lists of balances extracted from the sales and purchases ledgers:
- **schedule of trade receivables** — a list of all the debit balances extracted from the sales ledger
- **schedule of trade payables** — a list of all the credit balances extracted from the purchases ledger

Credit balances in the sales ledger must not be netted out with the debit balances. Debit balances in the purchases ledger must not be netted out with the credit balances.

The total of the schedule of trade receivables should equal the debit balance shown in the sales ledger control account. The total of the schedule of trade payables should equal the credit balance shown in the purchases ledger control account.

Preparing a control account

In a business that has a large number of credit customers and credit suppliers, there will be many entries made in the sales ledger and purchases ledger. This means that there is great potential for errors to be made. Control accounts are used to check the accuracy of the entries made in each of the sales ledgers and each of the purchases ledgers.

A control account is a summary of all the entries that have been made in each sales ledger and each purchases ledger in any particular month. Any entry in any sales ledger or purchases ledger is duplicated in the appropriate control account. Some businesses maintain control accounts as part of their double-entry system, while others maintain the control accounts as memorandum accounts. For the purposes of the examination, there is no difference in their preparation.

Examples:

Sales ledger					Sales ledger control account			
Dr		B. Keaton		Cr	Dr			Cr
Balance b/d	123	Returns inward	57		Balance b/d	123 000	Returns inward	57 000
Sales	217	Cash	200		Sales	217 000	Cash	200 000
		Discount all'd	22				Discount all'd	22 000
		Balance c/d	61				Balance c/d	61 000
	340		340			340 000		340 000
Balance b/d	61					Balance b/d	61 000	

Follow the same principles when preparing a purchases ledger control account.

Remember that if an entry in the double-entry system does not appear in a personal ledger then it will not appear in a control account.

You should know where each of the figures used in a control account comes from. They all come from a total extracted from a subsidiary book. In the example above of a sales ledger control account:

Knowledge check 15

A list of balances extracted from a sales ledger shows debit balances £26 300 and credit balances £300. How should this information be shown in a trial balance?

Knowledge check 16

If a control account balances, this is proof that there are not errors in that particular ledger. True or false?

Examiner tip

The most common error students make when preparing a control account is to reverse all entries. Practise preparing individual accounts from the sales ledger and the purchases ledger – control accounts look similar but use larger amounts of money.

- sales £217 000 is the total of the credit sales recorded in the sales day book
- returns inward £57 000 is the total of the goods returned recorded in the sales returns day book
- cash £200 000 is the total of cash received from customers recorded in the cash book
- discount allowed £22 000 is the total of the discount allowed columns in the cash book

Summary

- A trial balance is prepared using information extracted from all three ledgers (and the cash book).
- It is a summarised version of all accounts found in all three ledgers.
- The debit column of a trial balance lists all assets and expenses.
- The credit column lists all liabilities, incomes and benefits.
- A trial balance checks the arithmetical accuracy of the whole double-entry system.
- It is also a convenient list that can be used to prepare a set of financial statements.
- If a trial balance balances, it is not a guarantee that the double-entry system is error free.
- There are six types of error that will not be disclosed by extracting a trial balance.
- If a trial balance does not balance, the difference is entered in a suspense account.
- When errors in the double-entry system are found, they are rectified by using the journal. Any corrected errors that are entered in a suspense account should cancel out the suspense account.
- Bank reconciliation statements are used to check the accuracy of entries in the bank columns of the cash book.

- Examination questions usually involve two parts:
  - the cash book is updated for any items that have been omitted or entered incorrectly
  - the actual reconciliation statement is prepared using the amended cash book balance and adjusted for unpresented cheques and lodgements not yet entered on the bank statement
- Control accounts help to find errors in the two personal ledgers.
- Control accounts are generally prepared each month for each individual personal ledger.
- All entries that appear in the sales ledger will appear in a sales ledger contol account: all entries that appear in a purchases ledger will appear in a purchases ledger control account.
- Bad debts written off in a sales ledger will appear on the credit side of a sales ledger control account; a provision for doubtful debts does not feature in a sales ledger control account.
- Transfers from one ledger to another are entered in the journal and from there into both ledgers and so both control accounts.
- Transfers (set-offs/contra items) are credited to the sales ledger control account and debited to the purchases ledger control account.

Income statements and statements of financial position

Income statements

You must be able to prepare income statements quickly and above all accurately from a trial balance, taking into account any additional information given in the question. To speed up your preparations of these accounts, practise marking alongside each item given in a trial balance: 'T' for trading section, 'P' for profit and loss section, and 'F' for statement of financial position. This can help when you start your answer. In most, if not all, examinations you will find a question that requires the preparation of:

- a trading section of an income statement or
- a profit and loss section of an income statement or
- an income statement showing both sections

You must practise the layout used by your teacher and in textbooks. Good layouts could be rewarded with a quality of presentation mark (or two).

Some items in trading sections that cause students problems include the following.

Examiner tip
Learn the income statement layout. Use full headings without abbreviations.

Headings

Always use a full heading. Do not abbreviate any part of the heading. The heading should include the business name. An example might be:

R. Rajan. Trading section of an income statement for the year ended 31 March 2012

Note that there are no abbreviations (except for the first name) in the title or the date.

Returns

Inset returns and extend the net sales and net purchases into the main body of your answer. For example:

A. Smith. Trading section of an income statement for the year ended 30 April 2012

	£	£	£
Sales		210 367	
Less returns inwards		1 248	209 119
Less cost of sales			
Inventory 1 May 2011		15 762	
Purchases	96 499		
Less returns outwards	634	95 865	
		111 627	
Inventory 30 April 2012		17 498	94 129
Gross profit			114 990

Note that 'gross profit' is written in full — abbreviating the words will cost you a mark — and that the cost of sales is identified.

Some people prefer to identify the cost of sales figure in the line above the gross profit.

**A. Smith. Trading section of an income statement for the year ended
30 April 2012**

	£	£	£
Sales			210 367
Less returns inwards			1 248
			209 119
Inventory 1 May 2011		15 762	
Purchases	96 499		
Less returns outwards	634	95 865	
		111 627	
Inventory 30 April 2012		17 498	
Cost of sales			94 129
Gross profit			114 990

This is equally acceptable as a layout. Choose the one you feel most comfortable using and use it always.

Goods taken out of the business

Goods taken out of the business for the use of the proprietor should not be included in the financial statements of the business so they are deducted from purchases. They must also be included as part of the owner's drawings. Show your calculation as workings. For example:

**R. Roy. Trading section of an income statement for the year ended
29 February 2012**

		£	£
Sales			72 488
Less cost of sales			
	Inventory 1 March 2011	748	
	Purchases	26 103	
		26 851	
	Inventory 29 February 2012	649	26 202
Gross profit			46 286

27 603 purchases less
1500 goods for own use

Carriage

Carriage inwards is shown as an addition to purchases, since carriage inwards makes the purchases more expensive. An example is given on the next page.

P. Lefevre. Trading section of an income statement for the year ended 31 March 2012

	£	£	£
Sales			143 003
Less cost of sales			
Inventory 1 April 2011		7 461	
Purchases	64 728		
Carriage inwards	643	65 371	
		72 832	
Inventory 31 March 2012		8 112	64 720
Gross profit			78 283

Carriage outwards is an expense that is shown in the profit and loss section.

A profit and loss section must also have a full heading. An example is:

A. Lim. Profit and loss section of an income statement for the year ended 31 January 2012

Note that there are no abbreviations in the title or the date.

Other items in a profit and loss section can cause problems to some students:

Accruals

The value of resources that are used to produce sales (and consequently profits) must be accounted for in the financial year of use, whether or not they have been paid for.

For example, wages amounting to £37 430 have been paid during the financial year (amount shown on trial balance). At the year end, wages amounting to £674 remain unpaid. £674 of workers' skills and expertise, although used during the financial year, have not yet been paid for by the business. This amount needs to be added to £37 430 to give the total use of resources during the year. The amount entered under expenses in the profit and loss section for wages is £38 104 (£37 430 + £674).

Prepayments

We are interested only in expenditure for the financial year in question. That is what our heading tells us: 'Profit and loss section of an income statement for the year...'. Any amounts paid for the next financial year must be disregarded.

For example, insurances amounting to £1794 have been paid during the financial year (amount shown on the trial balance). At the year end, insurances paid in advance (i.e. for the following financial year) amounted to £287. £287 has been paid for insurance for the following financial year and should be included in next year's profit and loss section as an expense. Only £1507 (£1794 – £287) should be shown in this year's financial statements.

Discounts

Discounts received increase profit for the year and so are added to the gross profit. Discount allowed is regarded as an expense. Although it is acceptable to net the cash

Knowledge check 18

A business makes a gross profit of £140 000 and a profit for the year of £76 000. Carriage inwards £400 has been entered in the profit and loss section of the income statement as an expense; carriage outwards £500 has been added to purchases in the trading section.

What will be the gross profit and profit for the year, after the errors have been corrected?

Examiner tip

Do the calculation carefully when adjusting for accruals and/or prepayments. Even if you do the calculation on your calculator, write down (as workings) exactly what you have done. If you make an error, you will probably then score part marks.

Knowledge check 19

A business has made a profit for the year of £16 780. At the financial year end, wages owed amounted to £456 and insurance £67 paid for the following financial year had not been taken into account when preparing the income statement for the year.

What is the correct profit for the year?

discounts and use only one figure in the profit and loss section instead of two, it is safer to show the two discounts separately. (You could make an error deducting one from the other.)

Provision for depreciation of non-current assets

Examiner tip

Only the change in the provision is shown in the profit and loss section of an income statement.

The value of any resources used to generate sales (and consequently profits) must be accounted for in the financial year of use. When a non-current asset is used to generate profits then a proportion of the cost of the asset is shown as an expense in the profit and loss section of the income statement.

Example:

| Provision for depreciation of office equipment at 31 December 2011 | £16000 |
| Provision for depreciation of office equipment at 31 December 2012 | £20000 |

The income statement for the year ended 31 December 2012 would show, under expenses, provision for depreciation of office equipment as £4000.

The provision at the start of the year will be shown in the trial balance. The provision at the end of the year will need to be calculated. For example:

- Vehicles at cost at 30 November 2012: £125000.
- Provision for depreciation of vehicles at 30 November 2011 (shown on trial balance): £24000. Provision for depreciation of vehicles is calculated using the straight-line method at 20% per annum.
- Provision for depreciation of vehicles for the year: 20% × £125000 = £25000.
- The amount to be shown as an expense in the profit and loss section of the income statement for the year ended 30 November 2012 is £25000.

Knowledge check 20

Depreciation is the money set aside each year so that non-current assets can be replaced when needed. True or false?

Examiners can make the calculation more difficult by including the purchase of further assets during the financial year. For example:
- Machinery at cost at 31 March 2010: £45000.
- Provision for depreciation of machinery at 31 March 2011 (shown on trial balance): £18000.
- Provision for depreciation of machinery is calculated using the straight-line method at 10% of machinery held at the year end.
- During October 2010 a new machine costing £17000 was purchased.
- Provision for depreciation of machinery at 31 March 2012: £24200.
- The amount shown as an expense in the income statement for the year ended 31 March 2012 is £6200 [(£45000 + £17000) × 10%].

The cost of a non-current asset less the aggregate (total) depreciation to date is known as the **carrying amount**.

Knowledge check 21

Explain the difference between non-current assets and current assets.

You must be able to prepare a statement of financial position in good form, quickly and accurately from a trial balance, taking into account any additional information given in the question. Make sure that you are able to classify assets into non-current and current assets and liabilities into non-current liabilities. Label the headings and do not use abbreviations.
- Non-current assets used to yield benefits for the business for more than 1 year.
- Current assets are cash or assets that are changed into cash within 1 year.
- Non-current liabilities are debts owed by a business that are due to be repaid in more than 1 year's time.
- Current liabilities are debts owed by a business that need to be repaid within 1 year.

Knowledge check 22

Explain the circumstances that would classify a five-year bank loan as a current liability.

Capital is the term used to describe how much a business is worth to the proprietor. It is also the amount of money that the owner has invested in the business. It is made up of the money that the owner has injected into the business, plus any profits reinvested over the business's lifetime, less any withdrawals of cash or goods (drawings) made over the years of ownership.

Knowledge check 23

Capital is the money held as cash and bank balances in a business. True or false?

You must also be able to close down the nominal accounts shown in a general ledger. In addition, you must be able to incorporate into these accounts any accruals and prepayments that may be outstanding at the end of the financial year.

Example:

The following rent account appears in the general ledger of a business at 31 December 2008.

Rent account

Dr				Cr
3 January	Bank	CB28	300	
28 April	Bank	CB47	300	
17 August	Bank	CB68	300	

The payment due on 1 October 2008 had not been paid at the financial year end, 31 December 2012. Rent is due quarterly on 1 January, 1 April, 1 July and 1 October.

Prepare the rent account as it would appear at the financial year end.

Answer:

At the year end £300 rent is owing. The safest way to prepare the account is to follow this procedure.

(1)

Rent account

Dr			Cr
3 Jan	Bank	300	
28 Apr	Bank	300	
17 Aug	Bank	300	

1 Jan Bal b/d 300

Showing £300 owing (a creditor)

(2)

Rent account

Dr			Cr
3 Jan	Bank	300	
28 Apr	Bank	300	
17 Aug	Bank	300	
31 Dec	Bank	300	

1 Jan Bal b/d 300

Take the credit 'back into the account' thus completing the double entry. A credit requires a corresponding debit.

(3) Add the 'heaviest' side and balance the account with a transfer to the profit and loss section of the income statement.

Rent account

Dr				Cr	
3 January	Bank	300			
28 April	Bank	300			
17 August	Bank	300			
31 December	Balance c/d	300	31 December income statement	1200	
		1200		1200	
			1 January Balance b/d	300	

So, rent £1200 appears as an expense in the income statement for the year. The credit balance £300 appears on the statement of financial position as a current liability.

A similar process is followed to record any prepayments in the general ledger.

Example:

At the financial year ended 31 December 2012, £150 has been paid for business rates due in the financial year ended 31 December 2013.

(1)

Rates account

Dr			Cr
14 July	Bank	900	
31 Oct	Bank	450	
7 Dec	Bank	600	
31 Dec Bal b/d	150		

Showing £150 prepaid (a debtor)

(2)

Rates account

Dr			Cr	
14 July	Bank	900		
31 Oct	Bank	450		
7 Dec	Bank	600		
			31 Dec Bal c/d	150
1 Jan Bal b/d	150			

Take the debit 'back into the account' thus completing the double entry.

(3) Add the 'heaviest' side and balance the account with a transfer to the profit and loss section of the income statement.

Rates account

Dr				Cr
14 July	Bank	900	31 December Income statement	1800
31 October	Bank	450	31 December Balance c/d	150
7 December	Bank	600		1950
		1950		
1 January Balance b/d		150		

Remember that the term 'debit balance' refers to the debit balance on the account at the start of the new accounting period and that the term 'credit balance' refers to the credit balance on the account at the start of the new accounting period. The safest way to ensure that you do not make an error is to always write in any balance 'underneath' the account and then transfer the same amount diagonally up into the account.

Also remember that the balances remaining on any account at the end of a financial year need to be shown on the statement of financial position at the end of an accounting period.

Bad debts

A bad debt occurs when a debtor cannot pay the amount that is owed. If it is known that a debtor cannot settle his/her account, then it would be inappropriate to leave a debit balance in the account since a debit balance on an account represents an asset. If the balance was left on the account:

- the total amount owed by trade receivables would be overstated
- the total amount of current assets shown on the statement of financial position would be overstated
- the total amount of all assets shown on the statement of financial position would be overstated
- the capital shown on the statement of financial position would be overstated

When it is certain that a debtor cannot settle the outstanding debt, the debit balance on the account cannot be allowed to remain for the reasons listed above. The debt must be written off:

- The bad debts account in the general ledger is debited.
- The customer's account in the sales ledger is credited.

The bad debts account is closed at the end of the financial year by transferring the total to the profit and loss section of an income statement.

Bad debts account

Dr			Cr
Arthur Baines	179	Income statement	809
Carol Dixon	83		
Gahir Jasdeep	135		
Elly Forsyth	412		
	809		809

In this unit you will not have to prepare the bad debts account, but the entries above show the process involved.

Knowledge check 24

Which type of ledger account is closed at the end of each financial year?

Knowledge check 25

Which of the following accounts should be closed at the end of a financial year: drawings; insurance; machinery; purchases; sales; Tom Smith a creditor; Vera Brown a debtor?

Knowledge check 26

Identify two real accounts that could be found in the ledger. State the ledger where they are found.

Knowledge check 27

Debts that have been outstanding for more than three months are always written off as bad. True or false?

Knowledge check 28

The owner of a business knows that trade receivables amounting to £670 will definitely not settle her debts. Which of the following statements is true?

- Business capital is overstated.
- Profit for the year is overstated.

- The trading section of an income statement is used to calculate the gross profit of a business by deducting cost of sales from sales revenue.
- Returns inwards are deducted from sales revenue to give net sales. Returns outwards are deducted from the cost of purchases.
- Both carriage inwards and carriage outwards are expenses.
- Carriage inwards makes purchases more expensive and is added to net purchases in the trading section of an income statement.
- Carriage outwards is a 'normal' expense that is entered in the profit and loss section of an income statement.
- The profit and loss section calculates the profit of the business net of all business expenses.
- Both parts of the income statement use only revenue receipts and revenue expenditure.
- Businesses account for the resources used during a financial year, not the money used to acquire those resources.

- The accruals concept recognises the difference between the actual payment of cash and the legal obligation to pay cash.
- The concept recognises the distinction between the actual receipt of cash and the legal right to receive cash.
- Accrued expenses are current liabilities. Prepayments are current assets. Cash received before a due date is a current liability. Cash due but unpaid to a business is a current asset.
- A statement of financial position is prepared on one day (usually the last day of a financial year). It shows the assets being used and liabilities owed by the business on that day.
- Liabilities represent the indebtedness of a business on the date of the statement of financial position.
- Capital represents the indebtedness of a business to its owner.
- Bad debts must be written off, otherwise the asset base of the business will be overstated and so the owner's capital will be overstated.

Questions & Answers

This section contains ten questions, each dealing with different topics in the unit. Each question is followed by two sample answers interspersed with comments from the examiner.

The questions are typical of those you could be faced with in your AS examination. They are based on the format of the AS examination papers. The usual pattern is that the first part of the question tests your ability to solve a numerical problem using knowledge, understanding and application skills. The second part of the question generally involves some analysis and then an evaluation of a scenario.

Sample answers

In each case, the first answer (by student A) is intended to show the type of response that would earn a grade A. Remember that a grade-A response does not mean that the answer is perfect. You will see that there is a range of marks that could score a grade A.

The answers given by student B illustrate the types of error that many weaker students tend to make and so deprive themselves of vital marks that could so easily have moved their script up a grade.

Resist the temptation to look at the answers before or during the answering of the question.

Examiner comments

Examiner comments on the questions are preceded by the icon ⓔ. They offer tips on what you need to do to gain full marks.

Examiner comments on the sample answers are preceded by the icon ⓔ. In some cases they are shown within the student's answer, but in the main they appear after the student's answer. In weaker answers, the comments point out areas for improvement and the types of common error found in answers that are around the pass/fail boundary.

Assessment

Remember that the course is designed to allow you to show your ability and to use your skills. AS, as well as A2, papers assess the following assessment objectives in the context of the specification content and skills. The following assessment objectives are tested in all examination papers to varying degrees:

- knowledge and understanding of the accounting principles, concepts and techniques within familiar and unfamiliar situations
- application of knowledge and understanding to familiar and unfamiliar situations
- analysis and evaluation by ordering, interpreting and analysing information using an appropriate format — making judgements, decisions and recommendations after assessing alternative courses of action

Quality of written communication (QWC)

On each paper, 4 marks are awarded for the quality of written communication. The marks are split equally between written communication (for prose answers) and quality of presentation (for numerical answers). These marks are awarded in specific questions that are clearly identified on the examination paper.

The specification requires that you use:
- text that is legible, and that your spelling, punctuation and grammar ensure that the meaning is clear
- a form and style of writing that is appropriate to the purpose and to the complex subject matter
- information in a clear and coherent way, and that specialist vocabulary is used where appropriate

Unit 1

The approximate weightings for Unit 1 are:

Knowledge and understanding	40%	29 marks
Application	50%	39 marks
Analysis and evaluation	10%	8 marks
	100%	76 marks (plus 4 marks for QWC)

The bulk of the marks available in Unit 1 are for the lower-level skills of knowledge, understanding and application (68 marks), while only 8 marks are allocated for the higher-level skills of analysis and evaluation.

You can learn to recognise the marks allocated to the skills of analysis and evaluation by the use of certain 'trigger' words. The most common trigger words are:
- Advise — suggest solutions to a problem and justify your solution.
- Analyse — identify the characteristics of the information given.
- Assess — make an informed judgement based on information supplied in the question.
- Discuss — present advantages and disadvantages or strengths and weaknesses of a particular line of action and arrive at a conclusion based on the question scenario.
- To what extent — similar to 'discuss' but requiring a judgement based on the likelihood of the potential outcomes and effects on the given scenario.

It is important that answers requiring analysis and evaluation result in a judgement being made. You use these skills almost every day. For example, you might say to friends, 'Let's have a McDonald's for lunch because...' — that is a judgement. You might add to that an analysis: '...because it is closer than Starbucks' or '...because there is a good offer at McDonald's at the moment'.

AQA AS Accounting

Question 1 **Source documents and subsidiary books**

ⓔ A comprehensive question testing a student's ability to trace a number of transactions from the starting point of a source document through to the debit and credit entry in the double entry system. It tests knowledge that is fundamental to the whole system of bookkeeping.

Complete the table below to show the subsidiary book in which the source document is entered and the accounts to be debited and credited. The first one has been done for you.

	Source document	Subsidiary book	Debit entry	Credit entry
1 Purchase of goods for resale	Purchases invoice	Purchases day book	Purchases	Supplier's account
2 Discount allowed to a credit customer				
3 Bank charges				
4 Unsuitable goods returned by credit customer				
5 Transfer of debit balance on Barker's account in sales ledger to Barker's account in the purchase ledger				
6 Goods paid for by cheque				
7 Invoice for the purchase of office equipment on credit				

(24 marks)

Student A

2 Cash book ✗a	Cash book ✓	Discount allowed ✓	Cash book ✗
3 Bank statement ✓	Cash book ✓	Bank charges ✓	Bank account ✓
4 Credit note ✓	Sales Ret. DB ✓	Sales returns ✓	Customer account ✓
5 Invoice ✗b	Journal ✓	Barker Sales ledger ✗	Barker Sales ledger ✓
6 Cheque stub ✓	Cash book ✓	Supplier's account ✓	Bank account ✓
7 Invoice ✓	Journal ✓	Office equipment ✓	Supplier's account ✓

ⓔ **20/24 marks awarded** This is a grade-A answer. The student succeeds in 20 out of the 24 responses.

a This part is rather tricky. The discount allowed would be offered on the sales invoice and so the response should be copy sales invoice. The discount columns in the cash book are memorandum columns — i.e. they are not part of the double-entry system — they help to collect all the discount entries. The discount allowed account is debited and the customer's account is credited.

b This part is also difficult. The transfer would be noted in a memorandum, probably instigated by a ledger clerk or by a credit controller. The account to be debited would be Barker's account in the purchases ledger. The student seems to have hedged his or her bets in this case, by giving the same answer for the debit entry and the credit entry. Alternative answers could have been debit purchases ledger control account and credit sales ledger control.

Student B

2 Cash book ✗a	Cash book ✓	Cash book ✗	Cash book ✗
3 Bank statement ✓b	Cash book ✓	Bank charges ✓	Cash book ✓
4 Credit note ✓	Returns day book ✗c	Sales returns ✓	Sales ✗
5 Invoices ✗	Sales day book and purchases day book ✗	Sales ledger ✗	Purchases ledger ✗d
6 Cheque book stub ✓	Cash book ✓	Supplier ✓	Cash book ✓
7 Journal ✗	Purchases day book ✗e	Office equipment ✓	Fixed asset account ✗

e **12/24 marks awarded** This is a grade-E answer. **a** The student knows that the discount allowed column appears in the cash book but does not realise that the double entry should debit the discount allowed account in the general ledger and credit the supplier's account.

b Although bank charges appear on the bank statement, the bank statement is not part of the records kept by a business. The bank statement is a copy of the bank's records sent to a customer of the bank.

c Returns day book is not precise enough. The student should identify the day book. He/she clearly knows that the credit note has been sent to the customer to record sales returns. Crediting sales would seem to indicate a further sale to the customer.

d This is a difficult part of the question. One of the uses to which the journal is put is to record inter-ledger transfers. The two accounts are reversed. The student ought to have cleared the debit balance on Barker's account in the sales ledger with a credit entry and then completed the double entry with a debit balance in Barker's account in the purchases ledger.

e The purchases day book is reserved for purchases of goods for resale. However, the student could have scored a mark by stating 'Analysed purchases day book'.

Question 2 Subsidiary books and ledger accounts

ⓔ This is an important question testing knowledge, understanding and application skills in a number of key areas. It has to be tackled with a systematic approach.

The accounts in the ledgers of C. Faraz, a trader, at 1 March 2012 show the following balances:

	£
Purchases	30 142
Sales	92 460
Carriage inwards	933
Returns inwards	2 163
Returns outwards	701
Inventory	2 968
Rent	4 400

The subsidiary books for March 2012 show:

	£
Sales day book	9 786
Purchases day book	3 466
Sales returns day book	820
Purchases returns day book	477

The journal has the following entry:

	Dr	Cr
	£	£
Carriage inwards	86	
Returns inwards		86

Additional information

(1) Carriage inwards entered in error as returns inwards.

(2) Rent remaining unpaid at 31 March 2012 was £400.

(3) Inventory at 31 March 2012 was £3420.

REQUIRED

(a) Enter the balances in the appropriate ledger accounts at 1 March 2012.   (7 marks)

(b) Make entries in the ledger accounts to record the information given for March 2012.   (8 marks)

(c) Make entries in the ledger accounts necessary to prepare an income statement for the year ended 31 March 2012. (7 marks)

(d) Prepare the trading section of an income statement for the year ended 31 March 2012. (9 marks)

(a)–(c)

Purchases account

Bal b/d	30 142	Income statement	33 608
PDB	3 466		
	33 608		33 608

Sales account

Income statement	102 246	Bal b/d	92 460
		SDB	9 786
	102 246		102 246

Carriage inwards

Bal b/d	933	Income statement	933

Returns inwards

Bal b/d	2163	Income statement	2983
SRDB	820		
	2983		2983

Returns outwards

		Balance b/d	701
Income statement	1178	PRDB	477
	1178		1178

Inventory

Closing inventory	3420	Opening inventory	2968

Rent

Bal b/d	4400	Income statement	4800
Bal c/d	400		
	4800		4800
		Bal b/d	400

ⓔ 17/22 marks awarded The marks are awarded as follows: 6/7 for (a), 5/8 for (b) and 6/7 for (c). The inventory account proves to be difficult for this student. The closing balance is entered correctly, but the opening balance should be entered as a debit and written off to the trading section of the income statement using a credit entry. The inter-account transfer from the journal has not been attempted. The other accounts are completed accurately.

(d)

C. Faraz. Trading section of the income statement
for the year ended 31 March 2012

	£	£	£
Sales			102 246
Returns inwards			2 983
			99 263
Less cost of sales			
Inventory		2 968	
Purchases	33 608		
Carriage inwards	933		
	34 541		
Returns outward	1 178	33 363	
		36 331	
Inventory		3 420	32 911
Gross profit			66 352

(e) **9/9 marks awarded** The answer to part (d) scores full marks. It is well laid out and accurate, using the student's own figures from part (b). The student has included the heading without abbreviations and the gross profit has been identified clearly.

(e) **Total: 26/31 marks (grade A)**

Student B

(a)–(c)

Purchases

Bal b/d	30 142		
PDB	3 466	IS	33 608

Sales

		Bal b/d	92 460
IS	102 246	SDB	9 786

Carriage inwards

Bal b/d	933	CI	86
		IS	847

Returns inwards

Bal b/d	2163	CI	86
		IS	2077

Returns outwards

PRDB	477	Bal b/d	701
IS	224		

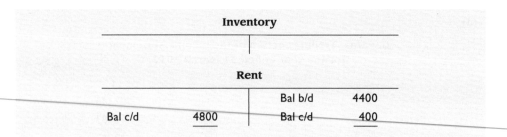

	Inventory		

	Rent		
		Bal b/d	4400
Bal c/d	4800	~~Bal c/d~~	400

ⓔ **12/22 marks awarded** The marks are awarded as follows: 5/7 for (a), 3/8 for (b) and 4/7 for (c). The purchases and sales accounts are prepared accurately. Both returns accounts contain errors, but are rewarded with 'own figure' marks in the trading section of the income statement.

The inter-account transfer from the journal shows two credit entries — only the entry in the returns inwards account scores. The rent account is reversed and the balance is not brought down. Remember that every debit needs a credit to complete the picture and that balances must always be brought down (unless the question tells you not to); otherwise you will always drop a mark.

(d)

C. Faraz. IS for y/e 31/3/12

	£	£	£
Sales			102 246
Returns inwards			2 077
			100 169
Less cost of sales			
Inventory		2 968	
Purchases	33 608		
Carriage inwards	847		
	32 761		
Returns outwards	224	32 985	
		35 953	
Inventory		3 240	32 713
GP			67 456

ⓔ **4/9 marks awarded** Here 4 marks are scored for sales, sales returns, opening inventory and purchases. The heading has too many abbreviations to gain the presentation mark — there should be no abbreviations. The description for gross profit has also been abbreviated. Carriage inwards is deducted and returns outwards are added.

ⓔ **Total: 16/31 marks (fail)**

Question 3 Income statements and statements of financial position

ⓔ This question requires the preparation of a set of financial statements with the added requirement of preparing four ledger accounts. It requires students to use the trial balance as a list from which the statements are prepared, which is a very popular type of AS question. There is the added complication of adjusting ledger accounts to take into account an accrued expense and a prepayment. Two bad debts also need to be taken into account.

The following balances have been extracted from the books of account of Linda Leigh after the preparation of the trading section of her income statement.

Balances at 31 December 2012

	£
Bank loan repayable 2019	15 000
Bank overdraft	1 369
Capital	47 824
Drawings	21 300
Equipment — at cost	72 000
— depreciation	27 000
General expenses	21 326
Gross profit	96 438
Motor expenses	8 612
Rent and rates	9 400
Inventory at 31 December 2012	12 400
Telephone	9 920
Trade payables	6 307
Trade receivables	9 472
Wages	56 116

Additional information at 31 December 2012

(1) Telephone rental £160 has been paid in advance.

(2) Wages due and unpaid amounted to £612.

(3) A schedule of trade receivables extracted from the sales ledger at 31 December 2012 shows:

	£
Bradbury	341
Mousaka	128
All other debtors	9003
	9472

The debts of Bradbury and Mousaka have been outstanding for well over 2 years and Linda has decided to write them off as bad.

REQUIRED

Prepare:

(a) the following accounts as they would appear after the preparation of the profit and loss section of an income statement for the year ended 31 December 2012 (open each account with the balance shown in the list above)

(i) Telephone account

(ii) Wages account

(iii) Bradbury

(iv) Mousaka   (12 marks)

(b) the profit and loss section of an income statement for the year ended
31 December 2012   (10 marks)

plus 1 mark for presentation

(c) an extract from the statement of financial position at 31 December 2012
showing current assets and current liabilities   (6 marks)

plus 1 mark for presentation

Student A

(a)

Telephone account

31 December Trial balance	9920	31 December Income statement	9760
		31 December Balance c/d	160
	9920		9920
1 January Balance b/d	160		

Wages account

31 December Trial balance	56 116	31 December Income statement	56 728
31 December Balance c/d	612		
	56 728		56 728
		1 January Balance b/d	612

Bradbury account

31 December Bal b/d	341	31 December Bad debts a/c	341
	341		341

Mousaka account

31 December Bal b/d	128	31 December Bad debts	128
	128		128

ⓔ **12/12 marks awarded** These are good, clear accounts. Remember that, if a question asks for accounts, they should contain as much detail as possible. Dates and descriptions are essential if you are to score maximum marks. Note that the student gives correct dates for the balances brought down, which start Linda's accounts off in the new year. (It is highly unlikely that folio references will be given.) One minor detail: headings for accounts in the general ledger do have the word 'account' in them, but it is not usual to use 'account' in the headings in the sales and purchases ledgers.

(b)

Linda Leigh. Income statement (profit and loss section) for the year ended 31 December 2012

	£	£	
Gross profit		96 438	
Less expenses			
General expenses	21 326		
Motor expenses	8 612		
Rent and rates	9 400		
Telephone	9 760		*wkg 9 920 − 160*
Wages	56 728		*wkg 56 116 + 612*
Bad debts	469		*wkg 341 + 128*
Depreciation	9 000	115 295	
Net ~~profit~~ loss		18 857	

ⓔ **11/11 marks awarded.** This is a perfect profit and loss section and scores maximum marks. Two points worth noting are: (i) the student provides workings (shown in italics) that are not absolutely necessary, since the working has been done in the accounts in part (a) of the answer. However, the student may have felt safer using this approach; (ii) the student realises that the profit is in fact a loss — the word 'profit' has been crossed out and the word 'loss' inserted. Do not alter figures or words: cross them out and write the new figure or word above or alongside. This will help both you and the examiner. The presentation mark is scored – the heading is perfect and the loss is described correctly.

(c)

Linda Leigh. Extract from the statement of financial position at 31 December 2012

	£	£
Current assets		
Inventory	12 400	
Trade receivables	9 003	
Prepayment – telephone	160	21 563
Current liabilities		
Trade payables	6 307	
Bank overdraft	1 369	
Accrued expenses–wages	612	8 288
Working capital		13 825

e 7/7 marks awarded The question asks you to show current assets and current liabilities. This student does all this and scores maximum marks, and also shows the working capital figure, which is not asked for, so the casting error is not penalised (working capital should be £13 275). Do not give an examiner an answer or part of an answer that is not asked for. The presentation mark is scored for the statement of financial position heading and the headings 'current assets' and 'current liabilities'. Notice also the use of the word 'extract' in the heading.

e Total: 30/30 marks (28 'accounting' marks plus 2 marks for presentation)

Student B

(a)

Telephone

TB	9920	Inc stat	9760
		Bal	160

Wages

TB	56 116	Inc stat	56 728
Bal	612		

Bradbury

Bal	341	Bad debt	341

Mousaka

bal	128	Bad debt	128

e 10/12 marks awarded The student showed a casual approach to answering this part of the question. However, the other 2 marks could have been gained by bringing down the accrual and prepayment balances. Remember to give all details in full. Once you get into this habit, it will become second nature to you and will ensure that you always score any presentation marks in a question.

(b)

L Lee. Income statement for the period ended 31 December 2012

	£	£
GP		96 438
Gen expenses	21 326	
Motor exp	8 612	
Rent	9 400	
Telephone	9 920	
Wages	56 116	
Depn	36 000	141 374
Pr		44 936

e **4/11 marks awarded** The heading contains three errors: the name is incorrect; the student has not prepared a full income statement, and has not prepared a trading section; and the profit and loss section is for the year (a period could be 2 hours, 20 weeks, 15 years etc.). The presentation marks are lost through the use of many abbreviations.

The adjustments made in part (a) are not followed through into the profit and loss section; depreciation is calculated incorrectly and the loss is described as a profit.

(c)

Current assets	
Inv	12 400
Tr rec	9 472
Wages	. 612

Current liabilities	
Tr pa'bles	6 307
Bank o/d	1 369
Telephone	160

e **3/7 marks awarded** Only inventory, trade payables and the bank overdraft are correct. The presentation mark is not gained: there is no statement of financial position heading, although the current assets and current liabilities headings are written in full. The accruals and prepayments are carelessly classified incorrectly. Trade receivables have not been adjusted to take into account the bad debts written off. With more care and more attention to detail the student could have obtained a higher mark.

e **Total: 17/30 marks (grade E)**

Question 4 **The cash book**

Questions on preparing a detailed cash book are common in this unit. Care is needed to put receipts and payments in the appropriate columns. Students must read the question details carefully, especially with regard to discounts. Sometimes the receipt or payment is given net of discount; on other occasions the student must undertake this task. The question requires the cash book to be balanced (and the balances carried down!) but students must remember that this instruction does not apply to the discount columns.

Carole Chung provides the following information for the week ended 31 October 2012. It has not been entered in her cash book.

24 October	Cash sales	528.65
25 October	Cheque received from Mitchel Ltd (discount allowed £29.78)	962.92
25 October	Cheque paid to Compo (discount received £5.60)	106.40
26 October	Cheque drawn for own private use	120.00
27 October	Rent paid by cash	80.00
27 October	Cash sales	745.88
28 October	Cash paid into bank	600.00
28 October	Dishonoured cheque returned by bank	73.87
30 October	Wages paid by cash	567.34
31 October	Overdraft interest charged by the bank	56.84

Additional information

On 24 October 2012 Carole's cash in hand amounted to £265.96, and she had a bank overdraft amounting to £3519.06.

REQUIRED

Prepare the cash book for the week ended 31 October 2012. Balance the cash book.

(20 marks)

plus 2 marks for presentation

Student A

Date	Details	Discount	Cash	Bank	Date	Details	Discount	Cash	Bank
24/10	Balance b/d		265.96		24/10	Balance b/d			3519.06
24/10	Sales		528.65		25/10	Compo	5.60		106.40
25/10	Mitchel Ltd	29.78		962.92	26/10	Drawings			120.00
27/10	Sales		745.88		27/10	Rent		80.00	
28/10	Bank C			600.00	28/10	Cash C		600.00	
28/10	Dishonoured cheque			73.87	30/10	Wages		567.34	
					31/10	Interest			56.84
31/10	Balance c/d			2165.51	31/10	Balance c/d		293.15	
		29.78	1540.49	3802.30			5.60	1540.49	3802.30
1/11	Balance b/d		293.15		1/11	Balance b/d			2165.51

ⓔ **20/22 marks awarded** This is a grade-A answer. The dishonoured cheque should be in the credit bank column and the descriptions for the transfer from cash to bank are incorrect. Remember that descriptions tell the user of the accounts where the 'other' entry can be located. However, the dates and descriptions are awarded the other presentation mark. It is good to see that the student has not balanced off the two discount columns.

Student B

Date	Details	Discount	Cash	Bank	Date	Details	Discount	Cash	Bank
24/10	Balance b/d		265.96		24/10				3519.06
24/10	Cash sales		528.65		24/10	Compo	5.60		112.00
25/10	Mitchel	29.78		992.70	24/10	Private			120.00
27/10	Cash sales		745.88		27/10	Rent			80.00
28/10	Bank			600	28/10	Cash			600
28/10	Dishonoured cheque			73.87	28/10	Wages		567.34	
					31/10	Interest			56.84
31/10	Bal c/d			2821.33	31/10	Bal c/d	24.18	973.15	
		29.78	1540.49	4487.90			29.78	1540.49	4487.90

ⓔ **10/22 marks awarded** The student does not reach the standard required for a pass grade. The answer contains many basic errors. The transactions involving Mitchel and Compo are incorrect — the question clearly states the amounts that were paid and received. The description for drawings is not penalised, since the amount is correct and, even though the description does not tell where the debit entry is, the principle is correct. The cash payment to bank incorrectly comes out of bank and is described incorrectly. It should also be written as 600.00, for clarity. The amounts are not penalised, but care should be taken as this type of careless entry can result in casting errors. The treatment of the dishonoured cheque is incorrect — it should be entered in the credit bank column. Rent has been entered incorrectly in the bank column. The discount column should not be balanced. Finally, a couple of marks are lost because all balances need to be brought down. One mark is scored for presentation as the dates are correct and the descriptions in the main are also correct.

Question 5 **The trial balance**

This question requires students to be able to prepare a trial balance quickly and accurately, and then use the information to prepare an income statement. Additionally, the student has to explain why a trial balance is prepared. Students must be familiar with using a report (and memorandum) format. It is important that students reach some conclusion when they are asked to discuss a topic.

Eric Hotler is a sole trader who owns a shop. The following information has been extracted from his books of account at 30 November 2012.

	£
Balance at bank	4 863
Bank loan repayable (2025)	25 000
Capital	12 244
Carriage inwards	453
Carriage outwards	656
Discounts allowed	830
Discounts received	1 008
Drawings	24 500
General expenses	18 769
Motor expenses	8 671
Purchases	167 919
Rent receivable	5 700
Returns inwards	275
Returns outwards	573
Sales	282 551
Inventory 1 December 2011	18 434
Trade payables	8 456
Trade receivables	1 763
Vehicle — at cost	32 000
Vehicle — depreciation to date	8 000
Wages	64 399

REQUIRED

(a) Prepare a trial balance using the balances shown above. (11 marks)

(b) Explain the function of preparing a trial balance. (3 marks)

Additional information to the trial balance

(1) Inventory at 30 November 2012 was valued at £18 648.

(2) During the year, Eric took goods from the business for his own private use valued at £300.

(3) Motor expenses due and unpaid amounted to £399 at 30 November 2012.

(4) Wages paid in advance amounted to £732 at 30 November 2012.

(5) Depreciation is to be provided on the vehicle at 25% using the straight-line method.

REQUIRED

(c) Prepare an income statement for the year ended 30 November 2012.   (20 marks)

plus 2 marks for presentation

**(d) Prepare a brief report addressed to Eric discussing the reasons
why a trader should prepare a set of financial statements.**   (7 marks)

plus 2 marks for quality of written communication

Student A

(a)

Trial balance at 30 November 2012

	Debit £	Credit £
Balance at bank	4863	
Bank loan (repayable 2025)		25000
Capital		12244
Carriage inwards	453	
Carriage outwards	656	
Discount allowed	830	
Discount received		1008
Drawings	24500	
General expenses	18769	
Motor expenses	8671	
Purchases	167919	
Rent received		5700
Returns inwards	275	
Returns outwards		573
Sales		282551
Inventory	18434	
T payables		8456
T receivables	1763	
Vehicle	24000	
Wages	64399	
	335532	335532

🄔 **10/11 marks awarded** This is a good answer. The heading is absolutely correct. The
layout is clear and accurate except for the entry for vehicle; the depreciation should not have
been deducted from the cost of the vehicle. Always show the asset at cost as a debit and the

accumulated depreciation separately as a credit entry. Information should always be shown in full — accounting is a medium of communication.

(b) A trial balance checks the arithmetic accuracy of all the entries in the ledgers and the cash book. It is also a great help when you have to prepare an income statement and a statement of financial position because you can get all the figures you need from one document.

ⓔ **3/3 marks awarded** This is a well-expressed answer. The student answers the question in the first sentence. The second sentence gives an additional use to which the trial balance can be put. Remember that there are no negative marks in any AS examination, so explain all written answers in as much detail as you know. If you write something that is incorrect, marks cannot be deducted from those that you have already scored.

(c)

Eric Hotler. Income statement for the year ended 30 November 2012

	£	£	£
Sales		282551	
Returns		275	282276	*wkgs*
Inventory		18434	
Purchases	167619		*167919 – 300*
Carriage in	453		
	168072		
Returns out	573		
		167499	
		185933	
Inventory		18648	
Cost of sales		167285	
Gross profit		114991	
Rent		5700	
Discount received		1008	
Less expenses		121699	
Discount allowed	830		
General expenses	18769		
Motor expenses	8272		*8671 – 399*
Wages	63667		*64399 – 732*
Depreciation	8000	99538	*32000 × 25%*
Profit		22161	

I have missed out carriage outwards. This should be an expense in the p and l section so my expenses should be £100194 and my profit should be £21505.

ⓔ **21/22 marks awarded** This answer has a clear layout, using inset figures to give the answer clarity. There are good workings alongside the figures that have been adjusted. The only error is that the accrued motor expenses have been deducted rather than being added to the trial balance figure. However, because workings have been shown, only 1 mark has been lost.

The student's own omission of the carriage outwards has been noticed and a note made to this effect. This is a good technique that will be rewarded. This type of note means that the original answer is not subject to many crossings out or alterations to figures that inevitably lead to further errors.

The quality of presentation scores both marks: the heading is perfect and all the labels are correct.

(d) REPORT
    To: Eric Hotler
    From: A Student
    Date: 4 December 2012
    Subject: Reasons for preparing financial statements
    Although you are not legally obliged to prepare sets of financial statements,
I believe that it is in your best interest to prepare them.

ⓔ This is a good opening sentence that sets the scene and summarises the discussion that follows.

    Accounts are prepared for two main reasons:
    1 For management purposes. You can see what are the good financial points shown in the financial statements and hopefully copy the good things into other parts of your business. You can also judge areas where economies might be made. For example, your motor expenses might include spending on petrol and your van may only be getting 4 miles to the litre. When you next change your vehicle you may find that your costs may go down if you buy a diesel vehicle which will give you more miles to the litre. You may also be able to get your purchases from a cheaper supplier. Are your wages too high? If so, you might be able to get rid of surplus staff. But do be careful that you don't upset the staff that are left.

ⓔ This paragraph is good and explains how Eric can manage his business more efficiently to save on business expenses. Although not expressed in perfect English, the student has communicated the information clearly and has given good examples.

    2 For stewardship reasons. People who invest in a business are usually interested to see if you are using their finance wisely. They can only do this by looking at the financial statements. You have borrowed money long term from his bank. I am sure that the bank manager will want to see the statements to make sure that his money is safe so that the interest can be paid on the loan and the loan can be paid back in 2025.

ⓔ This is another good paragraph. The student identifies a reason and develops it well using an example from the scenario of the question.

> Although sole traders do not, by law, have to produce a set of financial statements it pays them to. Because the tax man and the VAT people might want to see the statements to prove how much you owe them.

ⓔ **9/9 marks awarded** Although not written in excellent English, this is a valid observation, making it a sound answer that scores maximum marks — 7 marks for content plus 2 marks for quality of written communication.

ⓔ **Total: 43/45 marks (grade A)**

Student B

(a)

Trial balance for the year ended 30 November 2012

	Debit £	Credit £
Bank	4863	
Bank loan	25000	
Capital	12244	
Carriage in	453	
Carriage out		656
Discount allowed	830	
Discount received		1008
Drawings		24500
General expenses	18769	
Motor expenses	8671	
Purchases	167919	
Rent	5700	
Returns inwards	275	
Returns outwards		573
Sales		282551
Inventory	18434	
Payables		8456
Receivables	1763	
Vehicle	32000	
Depreciation		8000
Wages	64399	
Suspense (doesn't balance)		35576
	361320	361320

ⓔ **8/11 marks awarded** This response is badly laid out — none of the figures line up. Fortunately, the student has probably used a calculator to add each of the columns, so it is less important than if the calculation was done mentally. The student realises that the trial balance does not balance but has wasted time informing the examiner and calculating the difference between the two columns. The heading is incorrect and there are five errors.

(b) Trial balances that balance (unlike mine) prove that there are no mistakes in any of the ledgers. If the trial balance does balance they are very useful because you can just use the figures as a list to prepare your statements. The statements are the income statement and the statement of financial position. The statement of financial position is not really an account but you have to do one to prove that your accounts balance.

ⓔ **1/3 marks awarded** The student has not answered the question. He/she makes an attempt in the first sentence, but the statement is not true (remember CROPOC). The student scores a mark for the observation that the trial balance can be used as a list from which to prepare financial statements. The development is irrelevant to the question set.

(c)

Eric Hotler. Income statement for the year ended 30/11/12

	£	£
Sales	282 551	
Returns	573	283 124
Inventory	18 434	
Purchases	167 919	
Carriges	1 109	
Returns	275	
	169 303	
Inventory	18 348	
GP		132 769
Discounts		178
Rent	5 700	
Discount allowed	830	
General expenses	18 769	
Motor expenses	8 671	
Wages	64 399	
Depreciation	16 000	
Prof		18 578

ⓔ **11/22 marks awarded** The layout here could be much better. The heading does not score, as the date is abbreviated. Both descriptions of profit need to be written out in full. The returns are confused. The goods for own use should be deducted from purchases (the student reduces closing inventory by £300). Both carriages (spelled incorrectly despite appearing in the question) are added together and the inclusion of carriage outwards as an extraneous item means that an own figure for gross profit could not be rewarded. The netted discounts score 2 marks, but it is

generally safer from a student's point of view to show them separately so there is no possibility of a casting error. The cost of sales figure is not identified and the rent received is treated as an expense. The aggregate depreciation is charged to the profit and loss section. Only this year's provision should be charged.

(d) REPORT

> To: Mr Hotler
> From: A Student
> Date: 4 December
> Subject: Financial statements
> Dear Mr Hotler,
> I hope you are well. I am writing this report to you to tell you the reasons why you should prepare a set of financial statements.

(e) The first couple of lines of the report are superfluous and inappropriate to a report. They waste valuable time. The student should make relevant points immediately. In a report or a memorandum you may use bullet points, but remember that each point must be developed fully in order to gain maximum marks.

> You really need to prepare a set of statements so that you can see how you are doing. Also it is the law that you must. If you did not know how you were doing you could overspend and go bust. It might tell you how you could improve your business. It could show you where you are wasting money.

(e) The student is touching on the management function of preparing a set of financial statements. It is not well expressed, although they state 'see how well you are doing' and 'how you could improve your business'.

> I hope that you have found my reasons of benefit to you. Please get in touch if you would like me to give you further advice.
> I remain your good friend
> A Student

(e) **2/7 marks awarded** This is an inappropriate way to end a report. A brief summary and, if possible, a recommendation are the expected conclusions.

(e) **Total: 22/45 marks** Overall this is a rather a weak set of answers, and not up to AS standard. However, there are indications that, with more study and practice, a much better mark could be achieved.

Question 6 **Verifying accounting records: correcting errors**

ⓔ This is a testing question, especially the error in recording the discounts. Students are recommended to show two adjustments in the suspense account as it is usually safer than showing only one amount. The profit adjustment needs care and the 'direction' of adjustments must be made clear to the examiner.

The totals of Kurt Klinsmann's trial balance at 31 January 2012 did not agree. He entered the difference in the totals in a suspense account.

He has prepared a draft set of financial statements. The statements show Kurt's profit for the year as £43 714. On checking his books of account, he discovered the following errors.

(1) The purchases day book had been undercast by £100.

(2) A cheque paid for a van repair £937 had been entered on the credit of the bank column of the cash book as £973. No entry has been made in the general ledger.

(3) Rent £500 paid for November 2011 had been entered twice in the rent account.

(4) Discount allowed £139 had been entered in the credit of the discount received account as £193.

REQUIRED

(a) Make any entries in the suspense account to correct the errors.   (7 marks)

(b) Calculate the corrected profit for the year after correcting the errors.   (6 marks)

(c) Explain two types of error that are not revealed by preparing a trial balance. Give an example of each of the two types.   (6 marks)

plus 2 marks for quality of written communication

Student A

(a)

Suspense accounts

Rent	500	Purchases	100
Trial balance difference	905	Motor expenses	973
		Discounts (139 + 193)	332
	1405		1405

ⓔ **7/7 marks awarded** Maximum marks are scored here. However, the student would have been safer showing that 'motor expenses' are made up of two items £937 and £36 as he or she did for the 'discounts' entry. Remember to back up total figures with workings. Anything you have to key into your calculator should be shown in your answer.

(b)

	£
Profit as per draft accounts	43714
Purchases	(100)
Motor expenses	(973)
Rent	500
Discount	(332)
Corrected profit	42809

ⓔ **5/6 marks awarded** This is a good answer. The student does not use a heading. Remember, headings tell the examiner what you are preparing. The only numerical error is to include the whole of the correction for the van repair. In fact, only £937 affects profit; the other £36 alters the bank balance, so it does not appear on the profit and loss section of the income statement. Is this a genuine error or a transposition error because the figures are similar? Do take care when copying figures; transposition is so easy if you lose concentration.

(c) Complete reversal of entries is were, say, wages £500 is put on the debit of the cash book and in the credit of the wages account. Theres still a debit and credit using the same amount so it wont show up.

Original entry mistake like when £200 is put in the cash book for advertising instead of £20. £200 would go in the credit of the cash book and £200 would go in the debit of the advertising account in the general ledger.

ⓔ **7/8 marks awarded.** Although the language is not perfect, the student clearly knows what the chosen types of error are and gives two good examples, scoring maximum marks for content. Communication is good, but there are many spelling mistakes and poor grammar. Only I mark is awarded for quality of written communication.

ⓔ **Total: 19/21 marks (grade A)**

Student B

(a)

Suspense account

Motor expenses	937	Purchases	100
Discount allowed	139	Rent	500
Discount received	193	Discount allowed	139
		Discount received	193
		Trial balance difference	337
	1269		1269

ⓔ **2/7 marks awarded** The student is unsure of basic double-entry principles and scores only a mark for the purchases correction and an own figure mark for the trial balance difference.

Although the credit entries for discounts allowed and received are correct, both entries have been cancelled out by the same entries being made on the debit side of the account. Is the student hedging bets?

(b)

	£
Profit as per draft accounts	43 714
Purchases	(100)
Motor expenses	(973)
Rent	500
Discount allowed	139
Discount received	(193)
New profit	43 087

(e) **4/6 marks awarded** The student chooses the incorrect amount for motor expenses but the effect of the adjustments to the purchases account and the rent account have been made accurately. The benefit of showing the two entries for the discount adjustment is clear in this answer. If the student had netted out the figures and used only one figure (£54), no mark could have been awarded. Here, £193 scores a mark. The total gains an 'own figure' mark.

(c) Reversal entries putting rent into the motor expenses account doesn't make any difference the trial balance has got to balance.
   Corresponding entries where two entries are the same like heating and lightning.

(e) **1/8 marks awarded** One type of error is identified and scores a mark, but the explanations and examples are unclear and imprecise. No further marks are awarded. It is clear that the student should spend more time revising this topic.

(e) **Total: 7/21 marks (fail)**

Question 7 Verifying accounting records: preparing control accounts

ⓔ This question tests whether or not students are aware of the entries in both types of control account. Students are required to deal with a cheque that has been dishonoured by the bank. One entry does not require an entry in the control account and should be referred to. A discussion is required that needs a conclusion.

Brenda extracted a schedule of trade receivables for August from her sales ledger on 10 September.

The closing balance in the sales ledger control account at the end of August did not agree with the total of trade recevables for August, which was £14371.

The following errors have now been discovered:

(1) The sales day book was undercast by £1000.

(2) £246 recorded in the sales returns day book was actually returns outwards.

(3) Discounts allowed amounting to £461 have been totally omitted from the books of account.

(4) A cheque received from P. Arker for £720 has been credited to Parker's account.

(5) A cheque received in July from Garibaldi for £93 has been dishonoured. It was entered in the cash book in August but not in Garibaldi's account.

REQUIRED

(a) Prepare the sales ledger control account after correcting the errors. (10 marks)

(b) Discuss the benefits that Brenda would gain from maintaining control accounts. (9 marks)

plus 1 mark for quality of written communication

Student A

(a)

Corrected sales ledger control account — August

Sales	1 000	Discount allowed	461
Returns outwards	246		
Opening balance b/d	13 586	Balance c/d	14 371
	14 832		14 832
Balance b/d	14 371		

I have not recorded the P. Arker entry because it is only an error of commission.

ⓔ **7/10 marks awarded** This is a good answer. The only error is that the student does not adjust the total of the schedule of trade receivables to include the unrecorded discounts and the dishonoured cheque; the closing balance should be £14 003 (14 371 − 461 + 93). It is good to see that the student refers to the P. Arker entry (shown in italics). This dispels an examiner's fear that an item has been omitted because the student does not know how to adjust this error. The student earns a good mark for this testing question.

(b) Preparing control accounts will only disclose arithmetic errors in the ledger and in the control account. It will not show CROPOC errors which do not affect the balancing. So, someone looking at a control account that balances might think that it is bound to be absolutely correct. Also, a control account that does not balance tells the accountant that there is an error somewhere but not exactly where it is.

It will make the preparation of statements of financial position much easier and much faster. This is because the control accounts show the total trade receivables and trade payables at the end of every month.

It makes it much harder for people to fiddle the ledgers because the ledgers should be prepared by one person and the control account should be prepared by a senior member of staff.

I believe that Brenda should maintain control accounts because it will help to make sure that any errors in the ledgers are found and can be traced to a specific ledger.

@ **10/10 marks awarded** This is another comprehensive answer that covers the major points. Maximum marks are scored for content, with 1 mark for communicating the relevant points. Students must avoid colloquial expressions such as 'fiddle' and must not assume that examiners know what mnemonics stand for (e.g. CROPOC). It is good to see that the student has also drawn the discussion to a conclusion in the final paragraph.

@ **Total: 17/20 marks (grade A)**

Student B

(a)

Control account

Balance b/d	14 371	Discount allowed	461
Sales	1 000	P. Arker	720
Parker	720		
Returns	246	Balances c/d	15 196
	16 337		16 337

@ **4/10 marks awarded** 1 mark each is scored for sales, returns, discounts and the error of commission. The student could have scored 1 extra mark by bringing an 'own' trade receivables balance down to start off September's control account. Remember, always bring balances down; an account is incomplete if you do not follow this simple step.

(b) If a control account balances it means that the entries into the ledger are correct.
You can see easily the balances for receivables and payables so it makes the
preparation of a statement of financial position easier.
It will help to deter fraud.

e **5/10 marks awarded.** The second two points score marks. The first line is not correct. The comment about the preparation of the statement of financial position is succinct and scores 3 marks. An identification mark is awarded for the point regarding fraud, but this should have been expanded to explain how the preparation of control accounts can act as a deterrent. The student does not summarise the discussion. Although brief, the answer is awarded the communication mark.

e **Total: 9/20 marks (fail)**

Question 8 Verifying accounting records: bank reconciliation statements

This is a question that often poses problems for students. Two stages are necessary: first, to adjust the cash book to rectify any errors and to include items not already entered; second, the actual reconciliation statement. A memorandum format is necessary. The heading must not be vague. Only an explanation is required so no conclusion is necessary. Care should be taken to ensure that the 'quality' marks are earned.

The bank columns in the cash book of Diveron plastics show a debit balance of £1768.37 on 30 November 2012. The balance shown on the business bank statement on the same date did not agree with the cash book.

On checking the cash book and bank statement, the following were discovered:

(1) A cheque for £123.50 paid to Bloggs, a supplier, had been entered in the cash book as £132.50.

(2) A cheque paid to the telephone company for £627.48 had been entered in the cash book but had not yet been presented to the bank for payment.

(3) The bank had paid Diveron's annual subscription of £220 to the 'plastics' trade association' by standing order on 23 November 2012. The subscription had not been entered in the cash book.

(4) Bank charges of £37.22 for a temporary overdraft in October 2012 had not been entered in the cash book.

(5) The bank had credited the account with bank interest of £7.61 on 30 November 2012. This amount had not been entered in the cash book.

(6) Cash and cheques amounting to £1278.09 had been entered in the cash book and paid into the bank on 30 November 2012. These lodgements had not been entered on the bank statement.

(7) A cheque for £72.36 received from Harker and Co. on 18 November 2012 was entered in the cash book on that date. The cheque has been dishonoured by Harker's bank on 29 November 2012. No entries have been made in Diveron's books of account.

REQUIRED

(a) Make the necessary entries in the cash book of Diveron plastics to bring it up to date on 30 November 2012.
(8 marks)

(b) Prepare a bank reconciliation statement at 30 November 2012.
(5 marks)

(c) Draft a memorandum to the owner of Diveron plastics explaining the importance of preparing a bank reconciliation statement.
(6 marks)

plus 2 marks for quality of written communication

Student A

(a)

Cash book bank columns only

Balance b/d	1768.37	Subscription	220.00
Bloggs	9.00	Bank charges	37.22
Interest	7.61	Dishonoured cheque	72.36
		Balance c/d	1455.40
	1784.98		1784.98
Balance b/d	1455.40		

ⓔ **8/8 marks awarded** This is a good answer. The heading is clear and all the descriptions are as required. The balance has been brought down.

(b)

Bank reconciliation statement at 30 November 2012

	£
Balance at bank from the updated cash book	1455.40
Add unpresented cheques	627.48
	2082.88
Less not on bank statement	1278.09
Balance at bank as per bank statement	804.79

ⓔ **5/5 marks awarded** The heading is perfect and, although some of the wording used is not standard, it is clear and unambiguous.

(c) MEMORANDUM

To: the owner of Diveron plastics

From: A student

Date: 15 December 2012

Subject: Bank reconciliations

Doing a bank reconciliation checks the accuracy of the cash book entries for bank transactions. It shows where errors have been made like the mistake in entering Blogg's cheque.

It helps to update the cash book with items that the owner might have forgotten to enter in his cash book. Things like bank charges and standing orders. There are two examples in the case of Diveron: the subscription and the bank charges.

The bank reconciliation also checks the accuracy of the bank statement. Banks don't usually make mistakes but they could draw money out of the account by mistake or put someone else's money in.

ⓔ **5/8 marks awarded.** The student identifies three good reasons for preparing bank reconciliation statements. There could have been greater development in all three paragraphs by explaining how errors are located, how the subscriptions and bank charges are identified, and how withdrawals and deposits might end up in the wrong bank account. However, the student makes good use of examples taken from the question. Remember IDA: Identify the point, Develop the point, and Apply it to the question.

The memorandum format does not score as the subject is too vague. It should state 'the importance' or 'the benefits' of preparing a bank reconciliation statement. The remainder of the answer is well structured and clear, earning the further mark for communication.

ⓔ **Total: 18/21 marks (grade A)**

Student B

(a)

Cash book

Dishonoured cheque	72.36	Balance b/d	1768.37
		Bloggs	9.00
		Telephone	627.48
		Subscription	220.00
		Charges	37.22
Balance c/d	2597.32	Interest	7.61
	2669.68		2669.68

ⓔ **2/8 marks awarded** The student confuses the opening debit balance in the cash book with a debit balance shown on a bank statement (indicating an overdraft). The subscriptions and bank charges are dealt with correctly. The unpresented cheque is included and this extraneous item means that the closing balance does not attract a mark. A mark could be scored if the closing balance were brought down to start off the cash book on 1 December 2012.

(b)

Bank Rec.

	£
Bank overdraft in cash book	(2597.32)
Unpresented cheque	627.48
Lodgement	(1278.09)
Bank statement balance	3247.93 overdrawn

ⓔ **4/5 marks awarded** Only the heading does not attract a mark. The student's 'own figure' starts off the statement and, although the layout and descriptions are not perfect, the balance as per the bank statement is correct (using the student's own figure in the adjusted cash book).

(c) MEMORANDUM
   To: Diveron
   From: Me
   Date: 15 December 2012
   Subject: Bank recs
   It checks the cash book.
   It prevents fraud.
   It checks the bank.

e **1/8 marks awarded.** The memorandum format does not score. As with student A, the subject of the memorandum is vague. Also, the 'from' line does not reveal the sender of the memorandum. Do not be tempted to be smart either, so do not use 'Batman' or 'David Cameron' unless these are your names. The content is too brief but scores 1 mark. To gain further marks the examiner must be convinced that students do know what they are writing about. This can generally be done only if there is some good development.

e **Total: 7/21 marks (fail)**

Question 9 Income statements and statements of financial position

This is a 'standard' question with no hidden tricks. However, it does test the incorporation of an accrued expense and a prepayment. Depreciation must be calculated and treated accurately. Students are advised to practise the layout, with appropriate accurate descriptions, if they wish to gain the 'quality' marks.

Fred Beare owns a general store. The following trial balance has been extracted from his books of account.

Trial balance at 31 December 2012

	Debit £	Credit £
Bank overdraft		19614
Capital		79916
Carriage inwards	617	
Carriage outwards	2168	
Discounts allowed	412	
Discounts received		916
Drawings	39400	
Equipment — cost	74000	
— depreciation		37000
General expenses	42789	
Mortgage on premises		150000
Motor expenses	13628	
Premises at cost	200000	
Purchases	326490	
Rent and rates	9500	
Returns inwards	1380	
Sales		532461
Inventory at 1 January 2012	33418	
Trade payables		7988
Trade receivables	6480	
Wages	77613	
	827895	827895

Additional information at 31 December 2012

(1) Inventory was valued at £31907.

(2) Rent and rates paid in advance amounted to £600.

(3) Wages due and unpaid amounted to £877.

(4) Equipment is to be depreciated at 10% per annum using the straight-line method.

REQUIRED

(a) Prepare an income statement for the year ended 31 December 2012.

(22 marks)
plus I mark for quality of presentation

(b) Prepare a statement of financial position at 31 December 2008.

(13 marks)
plus I mark for quality of presentation

Student A

Fred Beare. Income statement for the year ended 31 December 2012

	£	£	£
Sales			532 461
Returns inwards			1 380
			531 081
Less cost of sales			
Inventory		33 418	
Purchases	326 490		
Carriage inwards	617	327 107	
		360 525	
Inventory		31 907	328 618
Gross profit			202 463
Discount received			916
			203 379
Expenses			
Carriage outwards		2 168	
Discount allowed		412	
Wages		78 490	
Motor expenses		13 628	
Rent and rates		8 900	
General expenses		42 789	
Depreciation		740	147 127
Profit for the year			56 252

ⓔ **19/23 marks awarded** This is an excellent answer. The layout is good and the student makes good use of insets, which help to show figures more clearly. There is, however, a lack of workings, which costs the student 2 marks. Two of the adjustments are made accurately and score 3 marks each, but the student drops 2 marks for not showing the workings: £74 000 × 10% = £740 is obviously an error, but two components of the calculation are correct and would score. Remember, always show detailed working for all figures that require you to do a calculation. The examiner cannot see inside your head or your calculator.

The presentation mark is awarded for clear labelling of the gross and net profit for the year and the heading, plus the identification of the cost of sales figure.

(b)

Statement of financial position at 31 December 2012

	£	£	£
Premises			200000
Equipment		74000	
Depn		37740	36260
Current assets			
Inventory		31907	
Trade receivables		6480	
Prepayment		600	
		38987	
Current liabilities			
T pay'bles	7988		
Bank o/d	19614		
Accrual	877	28479	10508
			246768
N C Liability			
Mortgage			150000
			96768
Capital			79916
Profit			56252
			136168
Drawings			39400
			96768

ⓔ **13/14 marks awarded** This is an almost perfect statement of financial position and earns the maximum 13 marks for content. However, the presentation mark is not scored, as the non-current asset heading is missing and 'non-current' is abbreviated in the heading for the mortgage on the premises. Avoid the use of abbreviations: they can cost you marks. Again, there is a good use of insets. A subtotal showing the value of non-current assets would be useful. The depreciation of premises scores because the student uses an 'own figure' from the income statement to arrive at the aggregate depreciation figure.

ⓔ **Total: 32/37 marks (grade A)**

Student B

(a)

Inc stat

	£
Sales	532 461
Rets in	1 380
	531 081
Inventory	33 418
Purchases	326 490
Carriage in	617
Carriage out	2 168
Less inventory	31 907
G P	200 295
Disc rec	916
	201 211
Less expenses	
Dis al	412
Wages	78 490
Motor expenses	13 628
Rent	9 500
Gen expenses	42 789
Depn	74 000
π	17 608

e **15/23 marks awarded** Although this answer has an unconventional layout, examiners are committed to rewarding correct content. Despite the poor presentation, much of the content is correct. A layout similar to that given by student A would make matters easier for both the student and the examiner. Carriage outwards has been entered in the trading section and a couple of adjustments are not made. An 'own figure' mark could score for the loss for the year, but the description is abbreviated (as a profit?). No presentation mark is awarded — the heading is not as required and descriptions are not written in full. The cost of sales is not identified.

(b)

SOFP for year end 31 December 12

Premises	200 000
Equip	74 000
Depn	74 000 ?
	200 000

CA		
Inv	31907	
Recs	6480	
Pbles	7988	
B/O	16914	
Mortgage	150000	
Capital		79916
Profit		17608
Drawings		39400 *ran out of time*

ⓔ **6/14 marks awarded** The student indicates that she/he has run out of time. In the time taken to scribble this, another item could have been put into the statement of financial position that might have scored another mark. This student earns 6 marks but 3 more marks could have been awarded by classifying the mortgage and indicating whether the 'profit' and the drawings had been added to or subtracted from the capital at 1 January 2012. Student B does not score a presentation mark.

ⓔ **Total: 21/37 marks**

Remember that an answer does not have to be perfect to score a pass mark or a grade A. The examiner wants to reward you for the knowledge and skills you have, not punish you for any mistakes. Student B scores a comfortable pass despite all the errors and inconsistencies, but could have done better by concentrating on layouts and stating whether items are added or subtracted.

Question 10 **Effect of errors on profit calculations**

The first part of the question is a fairly standard construction of a statement of financial position that students should treat as a different 'list' format. Part (b) is a different take on the usual question regarding errors not affecting the balancing of a trial balance.

Derek Baines has prepared the following statement of financial position for his business. Unfortunately, it contains several errors.

Derek Baines statement of financial position for the year ended 31 October 2012

	£	£	£
Non-current assets			210000
Current assets			
Inventory		13650	
Bank overdraft		2500	
Bank loan due to be repaid in 2012		100000	
Drawings		61200	
		177350	
Current liabilities			
Trade receivables	7000		
Trade payables	6500	13500	163850
			373850
Capital			108350
Profit			74500
Suspense account			191000
			373850

Additional information
- Wages amounting to £13000 had been included in drawings.
- During the financial year no entries had been made to record the following transactions:

(1) Non-current assets costing £34000 had been purchased on credit.

(2) Bad debts totalling £570 had been written off.

(3) A cheque for £650 had been dishonoured.

(4) Goods costing £750 had been sold on credit for £1000.

REQUIRED

(a) Prepare a corrected statement of financial position taking into account the additional information. (20 marks)

(b) Identify three types of error that might be present in the double-entry system which would not prevent a statement of financial position from balancing. (3 marks)

AQA AS Accounting

Student A

(a)

Derek Baines. Statement of financial position at 31 October 2012

		£	
Non-current assets		244 000	*210 000 + 34 000*
Current assets			
Inventory	12 900		*13 650 − 750*
Trade receivables	8 080		*7000 − 570 + 650 + 1000*
	20 980		
Current liabilities			
Trade payables	40 500		*6500 + 34 000*
Bank overdraft	3 150 43 650	(22 670)	*2500 + 650*
		221 330	
Non-current liability		100 000	
		121 330	
Capital		108 350	
Profit		61 180	*74 500 − 570 − 13 000 + 250*
		169 530	
Drawings		48 200	
		121 330	

(e) **20/20 marks awarded** This is an excellent answer and scores maximum marks. The statement of financial position is well laid out and is supplemented by clear, accurate workings.

(b) There could be an error in the statement of financial position that is cancelled out by an error in the income statement. For example, the non-current assets could be added to a total that is £100 too much and in the income statement the expenses could be underadded by £100. The statement of financial position would still balance but there are two mistakes, one in the income statement and one in the statement of financial position, but it would not show up.

Also, the purchase of a non-current asset. The invoice for it is lost so it is not recorded as a purchase and it is not recorded as a payable.

The income statement could be added up wrong say £10 too much and the statement of financial position could be added too much say the same £10. This would mean they would both balance.

(e) **2/3 marks awarded** The marks allocated plus the word 'identify' should indicate to students that the answer requires a one-word (or one brief phrase) answer. This student wastes time in writing in such detail and would have scored the same 2 marks simply by writing 'compensating

error' and 'error of omission'. The second example uses the words 'as a purchase'. Does the student believe that the purchase of a non-current asset is a form of revenue expenditure?

Take care to be clear when developing your answer. The third example given is a repeat of the compensating error.

 Total: 22/23 marks (grade A)

Student B

(a)

Statement of financial position for Derek Baines at 31 October 2012

Non-current assets			244000
Current assets			
Inventory		12900	
Trade receivables		7830	
		20730	
Current liabilities			
Trade payables	40500		
Bank o/d	2500	43000	
Working capital (minus)			(22270)
			221730
Capital			108350
Profit			74930 74500 − 570 + 1000
			183280
Less drawings			48200
			135080

 12/20 marks awarded This is a reasonable attempt. Showing more workings would have led to a higher score. Remember that any figure shown in the question that needs adjusting (no matter how simple the calculation appears to be) should always be backed up with workings shown on your answer booklet. Fortunately, the student does show workings for the profit figure.

(b) Addition errors.
     Putting non-current assets under the heading of current assets.
     Showing drawings as an expense in the income statement.
     All of these would still make the statement of financial position balance.

 0/3 marks awarded. The second two points here are examples, but the question asks for types of error not examples, so no marks awarded.

 Total: 12/23 marks (fail)

Knowledge check answers

1   The use of accounting information to aid managers to run the business more efficiently is known as the management function. The use of information to allow the providers of finance to see if their investment is being used wisely and is not at risk is known as the stewardship function. Management might use accounting information to determine if costs can be reduced by, say, moving premises to save rent or business rates, or changing utility providers.

2   Standing orders, direct debits, credit transfers, bank charges.

3   Purchases day book: debit purchases account in general ledger; credit supplier's account in purchases ledger.
Sales returns day book: debit sales returns account in general ledger; credit customer's account in sales ledger

4   True: Pawar's account will be found in the sales ledger.

5   For ease of use and to make the entries more manageable.

6   Debits: drawings, carriage outwards, rent payable
Credits: sales, returns outwards, discounts received
Closing inventory is not included in a trial balance unless the trial balance has been extracted after the preparation of a trading section to an income statement.

7   False. A trial balance lists all balances extracted from all ledgers.

8   An error of principle involves the entry of a transaction in the wrong class of account. It will affect the accuracy of an income statement and a statement of financial position. An error of commission does not affect the accuracy of either statement.

9   Commission, Reversal of entries, Omission, Principle, Original entry, and Compensating errors.

10   Sales: debit suspense £100
Advertising: debit suspense £10.

11   Gross profit reduced by £2320
Profit for the year reduced by £2500.

12   The bank statement entry is deemed to be correct. The bank columns in the cash book should be credited with a further £9.

13   £1308 credit (i.e. overdrawn) £1260 overdrawn plus standing order £48
(a)   Trial balance £1308 credit
(b)   Statement of financial position £1308 current liability.

14   £18 220 (£18 600 − £190 − £190).

15   The trial balance should show a debit entry £26 300, credit entry £300.

16   False: there could be errors of commission, reversal, omission, original entry, and compensating errors.

17   The amount should have been deducted from purchases. However, the correction will not affect the gross profit. This is an error of commission. So gross profit = £78 500.

18   Gross profit = £140 100 (£140 000 − £500 + £400). Profit for the year does not change since both are expenses.

19   £16 391 (£16 780 − £456 + £67).

20   False. Depreciation is the apportioning of the cost of the asset over each year of its useful life.

21   Non-current assets are held for more than 1 year and are held to help generate profits. They are not held primarily to be resold. Current assets are cash or will be turned into cash in the near future (i.e. within 12 months).

22   A five-year bank loan will become a current liability when it has less than 12 months before it has to be repaid.

23   Capital is not cash and bank balances. It represents the indebtedness of the business to the owner.

24   Nominal accounts are closed at the end of the financial year.

25   Drawings, insurance, purchases, sales would be closed at the financial year end.

26   Examples could include premises, machinery, vehicles, office equipment. They are found in the general ledger.

27   False. Debts are written off when it is certain that the debtor cannot settle the debt.

28   Both statements are true.